# The Theater of the Soul

# The Theater of the SOUL

## The Higher Self
## & Multi-Incarnational
## Exploration

SUSAN HARRIS

*Wind Horse*
PUBLICATIONS

Published by
**Wind Horse Publications**
P.O. Box 9939
Santa Fe, New Mexico 87504-9939

FIRST EDITION 1996

ISBN 0-9653413-0-5

**Publisher's Cataloging in Publication**

Harris, Susan, 1941-
    The theater of the soul : the higher self & multi-incarnational
exploration / Susan Harris.
    p. cm.
    Includes bibliographical references.
    ISBN 0-9653413-0-5


    1. Reincarnation therapy.  2. Spiritual healing.  3.
Consciousness.  4. Psychotherapy.  I. Title.

    RC489.R43H37 1996          616.89'14
                            QBI96-40250

*To my mother, Esther,*
*who knows how to honor the Inner Self and...*
*to my children, Monica, Aline, and Eli, the loves of my life.*

# Contents

⎯⎯⎯⎯⎯⎯⎯⎯⎯⎯ ∞ ⎯⎯⎯⎯⎯⎯⎯⎯⎯⎯

*Acknowledgments   ix*
*Foreword   xi*
*Introduction   xiii*


**PART ONE**
**The Higher Self**

Oneness   3
What is the Higher Self?   5
What is *not* the Higher Self   13
What's in the Way?   17
    *The Physical Body • The Mental Body • The Emotional Body*
Experiencing the Divine   31
    *The Inner Child • Contacting the Higher Self • It Takes Practice*

**PART TWO**
**Multi-Incarnational Exploration**

The Theater of the Soul   43
Reincarnation   45
What is Multi-Incarnational Therapy?   47
    *How It Works • Who Is It For? • How It Differs From Other*
    *Therapies • The Power of Love*
More than a Therapy   65
Consequences of Current Actions   71
Our Stories   73

## PART THREE
### The Higher Self in Life: Coming Home

Living It   89
The Power of Intention   91
Wake-up Call: Winds of Change   93
Surrender   97
Releasing Old Structures & Beliefs   103
> *Being Selfish  •  Rules of Life  •  Unworthiness  •  Religion or
> 'The Great Train Robbery'  •  Sexuality: The Silent Hum of the
> Cosmos*
Meditation, etc.   121
The Arts   125
The Infinite: Do We Dare?   135
> *Love  •  Awareness*
The Adventure   143


*Notes   147*
*The Network   149*

# Acknowledgments

———————⟨ထ⟩———————

U nlike a painting, many people can contribute to the creation of a book. It has been a great joy to see how the talent, skills, and support have come forward, just when I needed them. This synchronicity has helped me to realize this book has a life of its own, an impulse propelling it out into the world.

My biggest thanks goes to John Sumerlin, a man of infinite talents. Not only is his painting on the cover of the book, but he also came up with the phrase, 'theater of the soul.' He was my first editor, smoothing out the rough draft and helping to resurrect my basic knowledge of grammar. I value his loving friendship and support; they have been so important in my 'coming out' as a writer. Among his many talents, John is also a facilitator in Multi-Incarnational Therapy in the Boston area.

A big hug to Sandra Smith-Etigson, another dear friend who is herself a gifted writer and psychotherapist. She helped me further edit and shape the book, sculpting away unnecessary corners. I have fond memories of us putting our heads together one Saturday morning in her studio in Ruidoso, New Mexico not coming up for air until dinner. After that, the book felt complete.

Janice St Marie has been the graphic designer 'extraordinaire.' In discovering how well we worked together, words were hardly needed. How rare to find someone who is so tuned in to your vision and artistic sensibilities. As you can see, the final product is elegant and simple, embodying a peaceful feeling within its covers.

A special thanks to Mark Satz, who told me one Sunday after-noon last July that I needed to write a book on my work and philoso-phy. He said, 'It's time. People need to know about this powerful work.' He has continued to encourage and support me.

Now, to my children. Besides their enormous emotional sup-port, they have all shared their various technical skills. Aline, who put the book on computer and oversaw its production from my hand-written pages; Eli, who was called at 5:00 a.m. to rescue the book when it was lost in the computer; and Monica, who lent her skills at 'literary critique.'

Thanks also to our extended family here in Santa Fe. Jennifer Tambs, who saw the book through to the end, typing and editing, always with a sense of humor; and Kira Davis who was a graceful part of the typing network.

I have been so lucky...

# Foreword

I met Susan twenty-three years ago. We were at the first of many meetings of a Gestalt training group with twelve other psychotherapists. We learned much about one another during the next two years of training and began a lasting friendship. I moved to New Mexico and we saw each other rarely. Then one day in 1983, we ran into each other-literally-in the ladies room at La Posada in Santa Fe. Within moments we shared that we had both packed up our children, pets, and possessions and moved to Santa Fe, unbeknownst to each other. Thus began the deepening of our friendship and, for Susan, the beginnings of this book.

I was skeptical when Susan first began excitedly telling me about the powerful new work she was learning at the Light Institute. This was not a new feeling for me with Susan. I called her a 'scout.' She would trek out into new territory frequently as I watched with knitted brow and uncertain heart. Always, she returned, unharmed and wiser and I stored away her new found insights, with admiration for her persistent curiosity. This was different. She did not return. She kept searching and learning and I became a willing though still doubtful subject of 'past life' sessions.

It is my style to tentatively embrace the possible, which I did in the case of past lives. I did not exactly believe in this concept but I continued to entertain the possibility and eagerly set about to fit it into some conceptual framework that would explain the powerful effect the sessions had on me. I also sensed by then that Susan was not 'returning' from this particular journey and I had better figure it out.

The best 'framework' I came up with was that past life work gives us permission to broaden the field of our emotional/intellectual possibilities through our imagination in a way that we feel safe to explore ourselves truly with minimal fear and guilt. I had long been intrigued as a psychotherapist with how we use our imagination to heal and with how we use stories in that process. Past life work certainly addressed both of those aspects. This work helped me to vastly broaden the imagined scenarios of my existence. It was fun.

I have been privileged to hear the stories of many current lifetimes from my clients. And as these stories moved into the thousands, I began to understand that they are just that — stories. They are how we give meaning to our existence at any particular moment, how we attempt to justify and account for our lives. I began to ask people to just make up their life stories — not to worry whether they were true or not. It occurred to me that this is similar to what we do in past life work. However, in the framework of past lives, we have the freedom to create more imaginative and spectacular histories that reveal more and deeper wounds for us to heal. I have come to believe that the process and not the content of healing is what speaks to our neurons, transforms our cells and gives us nourishment on the journey back to our deepest and Highest Self. Slowly, over the years, the veils of my skepticism began to fall away as I remembered many unexplained experiences from my childhood and revisited poems I had written in early adulthood. Much of this made more sense in the context of past or multiple lifetimes. I also began to realize that my work as a psychotherapist was becoming more spiritual than psychological in nature, that reconnecting with the soul was the deepest work and healing the psyche was often simply a recursive intellectual exercise, like the lizard chasing its own tail.

In choosing to read this book I hope you, like me, believe that it is time to take giant steps, no longer baby ones, on our journey home to the soul.

— *Sandra Smith Etigson*
*May 1996*

# Introduction

I know of whence I speak. I have been through most of the experiences described in this book; from the depths of despair to the heights of ecstasy. I am not a newcomer to inner work, having done it all my life. At the age of ten, I was excited to learn there was a field of study called Psychology as I proceeded to check out every book on the subject in the Detroit Public Library. I have always had a great hunger and drive to understand human nature, myself included.

This drive took me into the intellectual realm, away from religion. At twelve, I resigned from the Jewish religion, telling my mother 'there is too much guilt and punishment in the stories we are reading in Sunday school.' I knew something was inherently wrong with that. I did explore other religious faiths, visiting my friends' churches as I grew older, but I found the same thing — even worse. I decided religion was definitely not for me after attending a catechism class with a college roommate who was marrying a Catholic boy and converting to Catholicism. In the class, the priest lectured about how evil the body and sexuality was and the need to have strict rules, governing relations between husbands and wives, which the church itself decided. I stormed out of that class and spent the rest of the night arguing with my roommate: 'How can you believe all that nonsense?' I was horrified, appalled and discouraged. Whatever church or religion I investigated all had the same message; guilt, punishment and denial of the Self.

I decided to become an atheist or at least an agnostic. That position proceeded for fifteen years until, at the age of thirty-five, I was 'dragged kicking and screaming' into spirituality. I did not seek it out, it found me. I could not deny what was staring me down, what was active in my life and in my psychotherapy practice. In counseling sessions with clients, there was 'something else' going on that I had no control over, a force orchestrating sessions so perfectly it took my breath away. Wisdom would rise up in me and the client; 'Who said that? Where did that come from?' There was a love, a compassion, an intelligence so present one could almost touch it.

So, I became a 'closet searcher,' reading esoteric and metaphysical books to the wee hours of the morning. Something was driving me to wake up and remember. Nothing else made any sense but this. And I knew what I was reading had nothing to do with traditional religions though some of the same issues were being addressed.

I didn't realize it then, back in 1975-80, that a new wave was sweeping the planet, a wave that was to transform consciousness. I have been thrilled to be a part of that; witnessing first-hand the fear, the trepidation, the shaking-up, the twists and turns of philosophy, metaphysics, psychology and science.It has been a whirlwind of experience I wouldn't have missed for the world! How lucky all of us have been who have participated in this shift of consciousness. What a romp and adventure! What a play!

Things are coming together now. Our consciousness has evolved to be able to understand paradoxes we couldn't conceive or assimilate before. Our brain capacity is not only enlarging but changing. The planetary shift is at hand and we are all a part of it. The shift is in remembering who we are: not as puny, sinful beings who need to be punished by a vindictive, separate God, but powerful, free, co-creators with the magnificent source we are all a part of.

Remembering involves the recognition that the 'play's the thing.' When I was going through my awakening, I had an 'awakening buddy' to share my excitement along with my fears. We would call each other at 2:00 a.m., talking in hushed tones about what we were reading and discovering. We 'cut our teeth' on the Seth book, *The Nature of Personal Reality* by Jane Roberts. This material blew both of us open to examine our personal belief systems. It particularly struck a chord in me, as I was beginning to come to the same conclusion with my clients: we create our own reality based on our underlying beliefs about ourselves and our perceptions of reality. Reality was not set in stone but could change as we change our consciousness.

My awakening buddy, Delmas, is also a gifted artist with a unique perspective on life. He has the capacity to step back from any current situation and see it all as the drama of life, He saw our clothing as costumes to have fun with, and our houses and furnishings as settings and stage props. It was all there for us to enjoy, experience and play with, but not to identify as our permanent reality. For his studio, he took first a large empty store and later an abandoned post-office and transformed them into movie stage sets with crystal chandeliers, paintings, murals, and tapestries. One was transported to other worlds when entering Delmas' studio, and it was the setting for art openings, the showing of foreign films, chamber music gatherings, poetry readings and elaborate costume parties. What a play we had! We even had a 'come as your favorite painting' party: imagination was free to fly...

When I moved to Santa Fe in 1983, I was ready to deepen my spiritual life and find a way to merge that awareness with my therapeutic work. Santa Fe was drawing me to it bosom; its adobe architecture, narrow streets, ancient wisdom and intense energy were calling to me. I moved there out of pure faith knowing no one, over the protests of my three children who thought 'mother is really going off the deep end this time.' I had no clue what form this next level of my life was going to take.

A year later I met Chris Griscom. Chills went up and down my spine as she talked about her work in opening 'the windows to the sky.' Chris was doing work to help people connect to their Higher Self and to explore their past-lives. She was also preparing to train people in this method and to open The Light Institute of Galisteo. At the time, I didn't know if I even believed in past-lives but I was so impressed that I made an appointment to see her. At the end of my first session,

I realized I had gone deeper and touched places that had not moved in twelve years of psychotherapy. Also, I connected to the exquisite love of the divine presence which was spirituality in its pure form, untainted by previous beliefs or structures. I knew then, that I wanted to train to do this work; this was what I had been looking for and why I had come to Santa Fe. This work wove together the emotional, physical and spiritual realms in a gentle, profound way.

The rest, as they say, is history. I was with the Light Institute for nine years, spending much of that time in Europe, eventually directing its European Center in France. I left the Light Institute when I felt the calling to integrate multi-incarnational work with my psychological/spiritual knowledge and to teach this method to people around the world. I am eternally grateful to Chris as a mentor, friend, gifted teacher and visionary.

Multi-Incarnational Therapy is a profound tool for personal transformation. It has touched me deeply; allowing me to clear and heal old conflicts, and to experience radiance and love I never imagined possible. I invite the reader to explore this method and hopefully, to gain a sense of this amazing process from this book.

I give it to you with great love...

— *Susan*
*July 1996*

*Part One*

The Higher Self

# Oneness

The idea of a vast subtle intelligence underlying and creating everything has been a fascinating and, at times, elusive concept to me. If we accept this premise as true, a whole field of questioning arises that may include, but goes beyond, our traditional notions of 'God.' It can challenge our basic beliefs about ourselves and even our physical reality. In fact, this inquiry often reveals more questions than answers. What does the concept of One Self really mean? More importantly, how does it translate into our daily lives? I sense that when we ask these questions, a radically different world opens up to us: a dimension of perception with a unique language, calling into play qualities we have barely touched upon as a species. We literally open the door and walk into a room we have never before been in. And we know it...

Increasingly, I have a sense of One Mind operating in the world. I notice how people give and receive messages simultaneously, and how as a global society we move jointly into areas of development and understanding. Individually, our physical and emotional needs are met by events we play out together intuitively, though we are often unaware of this synchronicity. It just happens. We think things at the same time. We are drawn or repelled to certain places and events like magnets. It certainly feels as if there is an invisible force at play. We think we are in charge of our lives, that we know what's best for us; but often circumstances are orchestrated to show us our folly. Needs and desires seem to arise from an emotional center which is limited by past beliefs and experiences.

What is, in fact, guiding our lives has a much richer perspective than we could possibly envision. In reality, it is the bigger picture. When aligned with this expanded consciousness, we experience tremendous power, peace and love. A view of life emerges allowing us to see ourselves and our dramas with compassion and purpose.

This is probably why humankind has felt so small and insignificant when contemplating divine intelligence. We haven't understood that this magnificence was our own substance, spinning our atoms. Our polarity brains have had difficulty holding the idea of paradox: we are small, yet vast at the same time. It seems that as our species matures, so does our capacity to understand truth. At times I feel my experience is of someone marginally retarded. I can glimpse what I don't know, with the awareness that my brain connections just aren't there (yet). I have come to realize with my own process, that understanding comes by being **one** with this presence, not by trying to figure it out. This has to be experienced directly.

I sometimes think of the physical body as a metaphor of our separation. Do hands and feet, fingers and toes think they are independent, that they are in charge? Are they aware of the rest of the body? What about the heart or liver? Is there consciousness of the other parts of the body, or of the brain which directs its operations? We each feel independent, separate but is that really so?

I feel a great sense of awe as I confront these greatest of issues rather than the insecurities and conflicts on which I have focused for most of my life. Often, I feel like running out into the street and stopping cars to say to people: 'Don't you know we're going to die? Don't you want to know what we're doing here, what this is all about? Who is guiding the show? And what is the show?'

So, who or what is the One Self? I have no answers. I only know that I feel it more and more. I see it looking back at me in people's eyes. I am aware of it being the 'doer' in my life, not me. I witness the miracles of its perfection and I am awe-struck. It fits none of my old paradigms. It is new. I am new. We are new. Very frightening... and very exciting...

# What is the Higher Self?

―――――――――――――――――――――――――――⟳―――――――――――――――――――――――――――

*'Truth is within ourselves,*
*There is an inmost center in us all,*
*Where the Truth abides in fullness; and to know,*
*Rather consists in opening out a way*
*Whence the **imprisoned splendor** may escape...'*
— Robert Browning

A love lives inside us, more powerful than anything we could ever imagine. A beingness that transcends all concepts. A flow of energy that can be tender, loving and compassionate and which can also create agitation and chaos. It is the force of the Universe, the intelligence that is all, knows all. It is utterly incomprehensible and totally available.

This force is called the **Higher Self**, because it is who we are at the core of our being, at our most essential level. It is the part of us that is aligned with and in communion with cosmic intelligence, while simultaneously having an experience in human form. It creates the uniqueness that is us, moment to moment, continually pushing us to remember our true nature as divinity. It holds a frequency of love that is unimaginable to us. In fact, love is its substance, no matter the appearance. The Higher Self is the wonderful mystery of the Universe — All That Is — God. Call it whatever you like. It is here. We are it. We have never been anything else.

When we talk about the Higher Self, there is an inference of its opposite, a Lower Self. While this appears to be a polarity, in reality it is not. It is simply a way to begin to describe an awareness that we are so much more than we have thought:

> *There are more things in heaven and earth, Horatio,*
> *Than are dreamt of in your philosophy...*
> — William Shakespeare
> *Hamlet*

There is only One Self, taking on different forms in order to have an experience of consciousness. The term Higher Self refers to the aspect of us that is always connected to source.

This inner presence never leaves us; never judges or condemns. It whispers to us, trying to awaken us to truth and to learn from the dramas it has created for us. This gentle strength is there to support us when no one else is there. It brings us into this life — creates the scenarios for us to learn, and takes us out of this life. It is with us every moment as our best friend, our truest lover, warning us of danger and guiding us to teachers and situations that will enhance our lives. It manifests whatever we need, always encouraging us to enjoy this great playground called Earth that has been created for us.

In fact, the eternal force loves to play, play being its forte. From its infinite abundance, it pulsates towards expression and expansion, always fresh, new and exciting. The adventure here is one of awareness: humans having an experience of separation in order to learn we have never really been separate, then choosing to see who we really are. Separation is the fall from the Garden of Eden, a fall we have all experienced. Awakening to our true Self is the healing. It is the coming home! It is the simplest thing in the world, and the most difficult.

## WHERE IS IT?

We have searched endlessly for the experiences that flow from connection to our divine nature: security, love, power, peace and happiness. Based on the mistaken belief that these are to be found in the outside world, we have tried various paths; the attainment of wealth, success, power and prestige. We've explored relationships, physical beauty, therapy, sports and gurus. We are like rats lost in a maze while trying to find the cheese. Even when the cheese has been taken away, we keep going down the same path. We are sure 'it' will be there if we just try harder, or if we are more worthy. This attitude becomes an endless cycle, which has led many of us to resonate with the Peggy Lee song, *'Is That All There Is?'*. Hopelessness and frustration accompany this lament.

Could it be that we have been looking in the wrong places, that we have been looking outside of ourselves for this happiness? Could it be 'it' is not something to be captured, attained, possessed or earned? Could so much we have been taught by our parents, teachers and the larger culture be wrong? That's pretty hard for us to swallow.

If we throw all this out, where are we? The whole structure of our lives has centered around the achievement of something outside ourselves that we believe is necessary to our survival, both physical and emotional. Our outward attention is continually being reinforced by the larger culture in which we live and our belief systems spin around this premise. Advertising campaigns manipulate us into believing we are in a continual state of lack that only their products can remedy. If we're unhealthy, we're told to medicate ourselves. If we're unhappy, we're told (or shown) to deny these feelings, or to cover them up with chemicals or activities. We are fed the notion that competition is healthy and that 'survival is the bottom line.'

We end up being more concerned with what people do than who they are. We scorn the poor and exalt the rich and famous. Being beautiful has become a cult. We have become a civilization that has made an art form of the superficial.

Yet, it is all we know. To reject these activities and their underlying values can be disturbing. What do we put in their place? Somehow we know deep inside that we have veered off track, though we can hardly admit it to ourselves; but this knowing resonates as a deep ache inside us. We feel shame at having betrayed ourselves, at having turned so completely from our own hearts.

The truth is, we are living our lives for the wrong reasons, to try to fill the emptiness inside us. While our activities can distract and temporarily amuse us, we always come back to the self which feels lost, confused, inadequate and scared. Addictions abound. We are desperate to find love, peace and happiness.

And now the good news, 'it' is right here, right now. It has never been anywhere else. It is beating our hearts, breathing us, thinking us, creating our bodies and orchestrating our lives. The 'it' we have been searching for is inside us patiently waiting to be acknowledged, waiting for us to see it, feel it and be it. So simple. We have truly been looking in the wrong places.

## THE YEARNING

We have been trying to 'go home' since we were born. From the womb we have direct memories of an inner stillness where all our needs were met. We also have recollections of a deeper silence, radiance and love to which we were once connected and have been trying to return. Who among us did not identify with E.T. when he pointed his finger upwards, and said 'home' with tears in his eyes.

This feeling of being separate has been our greatest sorrow as human beings. As children, we looked around and saw separate bodies acting independently from each other. It seemed logical to assume that we were all separate. Our focus was on our parents and the environment in order to ensure our physical survival. What our parents said or did was much more important to us than our own inner voice: our parents were our 'Gods.' Cultural beliefs and activities then proceeded to draw us further away from this Inner Self, towards focusing on the outside, and we lost touch with that presence, that precious connection with our divine wholeness.

We have spent our lives seeking this feeling of home, seeking connectedness to unconditional love, power and beauty. It has called to us like a long forgotten muse, 'I am here: come home.'

We remembered the frequency and have tried to mimic it in the only ways we knew.

The ecstatic current became translated into the pursuit of pleasure and excitement. The need for peace caused us to move away from pain and conflict into denial and a cover-up of our feelings. Our essential power and wholeness was often played out in tyrannical authority and arrogance. Inner balance and harmony were diverted into worship of physical beauty.

And love: that has been the feeling we most long for and most twist ourselves in order to get. Seeing love as coming only from outside ourselves, we have tried desperately to please others and be what they need us to be. This has led us to focus our attention away from our innermost needs and desires. Comfort and approval did seem to come from the outside when we behaved in certain proscribed ways: if we were good, unselfish, pretty, smart or successful. We listened to and trusted the adults around us. Unfortunately they directed us away from our Inner Self until it became a stranger to us. We never dreamed that what we were searching for was within our own being.

As a result, we have associated certain activities with satisfaction of our physical and emotional needs. This thinking has caused us to become addicted to just about everything: food, drugs, alcohol, cigarettes, cars, sports, sex, relationships, clothes, shopping, music, nature, fitness, working, television, movies, etc. — ways we have found to have at least an inkling of the divine frequencies we dimly remember and are trying to recover. With these activities we can experience a feeling of peace, joy, excitement and love, if only for a little while. One can look in any newspaper and see the notices for Alcoholics Anonymous, Overeater's Anonymous, Relationships Anonymous, Sex Anonymous and other similar groups. We are a nation of addicts!

But we are not sick or stupid, just misguided. We are trying to get home to what we know can nourish and sustain us.

We have turned to gurus and teachers to find the wisdom that can guide us back home, but most often we missed their message of looking inside ourselves to find the inner teacher. Instead we insisted on worshipping the external teachers, making them our gods. Even Christ said, 'You can do what I can do, and more...' We constantly externalize our experience, assuming the truth has to be outside ourselves. That addiction is perhaps the worst all.

## END OF THE SEARCH

We **are** the Divine Self. We contain everything we have been searching for so relentlessly on the outside. Within our own hearts is the most exquisite love and fullness we could ever imagine. In this place an incredible sense of beauty and well-being awaits us. For no reason joy rises spontaneously simply as an outpouring of this inner fountain of light. Creativity and knowing pours forth effortlessly; a vitality emerges that energizes and refreshes us continually. As we remember our true identity as love itself, the pain of separation starts to fall away. There is no death, no need to fear anything. Worry is unnecessary — something far beyond us is in charge and we know we are a part of this magnificent intelligence. We are connected to the greatest power there could ever be. It is **we**. We are the divine intelligence, the spiritual essence, that has taken on human form to have an experience. For now, that form has our name.

We're talking about a Higher Self that is our 'hotline to God,' that is a greater, more vast sense of who we normally feel ourselves to be. An expansive awareness that knows all, loves all... is all. It is we, only much, much deeper; we, in our finest moments and in our worst moments: ever present whatever the mood or circumstance; not ever gone, just usually clouded over, unrecognized or devalued.

Amazing, isn't it? What we want most, we already have. Yet in practice, we ignore it, reject and abandon it.

We're an interesting species.

## COULD THIS BE ME?

It is not hard to know the Self, it is the most natural thing in the world. What is hard, is getting underneath the thoughts and self-concepts of guilt and unworthiness that portray the individual self as evil, bad, certainly not 'holy.' We have believed so many lies about ourselves that we can't possibly think of ourselves as 'God-like' or containing the essence of divine nature.

Even if we can conceive of a Higher Self intellectually, the opposite beliefs lie buried in the cells of our bodies, out of our awareness. We have taken on the falsehoods of our planetary history, believed them to be true, and passed them on to our children. We truly believe that deep inside us we are sinful, not pure and good.

However, we do know the Higher Self intimately, all of us. We call it 'inner wisdom' or 'knowing,' a 'gut feeling,' 'common sense,' 'intuition,' or we say 'it just feels right.' It is the heart of us that knows what we need, if we stop and check inside. It is the knower, the seer, the lover. It sometimes talks to us, but most often we are aware of it as 'a feeling sense.' The presence 'closer to us than breathing, nearer than hands and feet.'

When we are in love, we particularly feel its energy. Our hearts expand with joy and fullness. Everything is perfect; we have a sense of total well-being. Judgment is suspended. Every moment is magical, exciting.

We know its ecstatic vibration at special moments through:

- The radiant smile of an infant
- The open hearts at Christmastime
- An act of kindness, compassion
- The merging of hearts in lovemaking
  and/or deep friendships
- The excitement and energy of our dreams, or new projects
- The forces of nature, it's cycles and
  rhythms; the wind that moves the trees
- Creativity, imagination, poetry, music, art
- A beautiful sunset
- Coincidence/synchronicity

These experiences inspire the heart to open up, to feel joy and ecstasy. We feel alive, connected, full, expansive. They are our peak experiences that create the meaning of our lives. But these feelings seem to come and go, to be dependent on accident or outside circumstance. They are wonderful, but certainly not dependable. Often we are left frustrated and confused. Our daily life appears bleak and empty in comparison.

ⓔⓔⓔ

This book is about understanding how to know the Higher Self as a continuous current of wisdom, love and power in our lives. How to call it in, be at one with it. To truly know the Self, easily, ecstatically. If we had known how easy it was, the planet would not have gone through the destructiveness it has. We are now in a remarkable position to change that. One can't control or intimidate people who are connected to their divine nature. There can be no wish to dominate or hurt others when we know them to be the same Self.

# What is *not* the Higher Self

O ne of the reasons we have so much trouble trusting our Higher Self is because of the chorus of voices going on inside our heads — many of which are telling us how bad we are, that we deserve to be punished. These voices talk endlessly at us. When we try to commune with our concept of 'God' or divine presence, an old frame of reference gets activated, bringing in the entire planet's history of religious thinking. Whether or not we are conscious of these archaic beliefs, they travel in our DNA and sit there affecting us, most often out of our awareness.

From the beginning of time, we humans have tried to make sense out of our experience here. Working with a primitive brain, we formulated religions modeled after our own human behavior. Most often what emerged was a spiritual framework based on a punishing God, or Gods, that we had to appease, or something terrible would happen to us. We projected onto these Gods our own polarity thinking and self-judgment and just about perfected the idea of blame as a reasonable approach to life; good/bad, right/wrong, black/white, male/female. All of these ideas led to a feeling of **separation** from ourselves and others.

Judgment became the rule of the land and of the households. Out of this judgment arose the most pernicious thinking which has eroded the emotional and spiritual well-being of this planet; a thinking that promotes unworthiness and denial of the Self. This attitude of separation has created beliefs, ideas, behaviors and thought forms that condemn and judge others. People are persecuted or ostracized when they don't conform, or when they are physically different. There has developed the virtue of 'being right' according to external authorities. Some of the origins of these 'rights' and 'wrongs' have become occluded over time, but they are still screaming at us.

I'm not criticizing rational human justice systems. They are necessary. I'm talking about thought forms and ideas that create guilt and hate. I'm talking about churches, educational systems and governments that are based on the denial of the Self's essential worth, wisdom and power, giving away this power to an outside authority.

It is this projected authority, or 'hungry ghosts,' that we encounter when we try to go inside our own being. The judgments of the ages come down on our heads, individually and collectively. Energetically, we feel this as a heaviness; they bring us down, make us feel bad.

I once asked a client to bring in his Higher Self. He saw a stern male figure carrying a balance of weights and measures. The message was: 'You deserve to be punished, you have been bad.' I gently assured him this was not his Higher Self and encouraged him to ask again. This time he had an awareness of golden light that was infinitely tender and loving. Enveloped by this light, he was told: 'I am always here for you, there is no judgment, there never was.' This client, a former Catholic, sobbed as he was able to embrace the real teaching of Christ, unconditional love.

We sometimes carry a fear of this divine force which sits inside us and is so readily available. It's as if somehow direct communication is not for us 'average people,' but for the priests, saints, rabbis and gurus. It is believed to be beyond our understanding, or dangerous somehow in the wrong hands. A client once told me she was afraid to 'use it too much, I might bother it.' We hold a belief that somehow profound love, joy, wisdom and ecstasy is not for the masses; that it is only available to a select few: those who have earned it, or have been blessed in a special way.

That kind of thinking is such hogwash! But we have believed it.

We have believed the authorities; we thought they knew the truth. Tragically we have believed in our own unworthiness and separation from the only force that holds any meaning.

But it is so easy. The time is now to see who has always been here, who has never gone away, and who has never judged us. It is looking out of our eyes — every single moment. Is it possible? Yes it is. It is here — **we are it**. The truth is:

- It has never been outside us.
- We don't have to earn it, or prove ourselves worthy.
- It does not take work or study. (Except to remove what's in the way.)
- We don't have to go anywhere to find it.

We just have to look in the mirror and see who looks back at us. The inner being — who never dies — who is connected to All That Is; right here, right now.

We only need to remove the veil of judgment and fear so we can hear, feel and commune with our innermost heart. When we do connect, the energy is happy and ecstatic. We feel uplifted, inspired and loved. It never, ever judges, only loves; because that is what we are, what the Universe is — only love.

# What's in the Way?

Our human experience is focused around identification with the notion 'I am,' from which flows association with thoughts, emotions, and physical sensations. When truth becomes only what we can see, touch, feel, or smell, we move away from communion with the invisible essence that existed prior to our birth. In order to reconnect to source, we're going to have to expand our sense of what is real and true for us, which can then open the way back to re-identifying with our true Eternal Self.

From ancient spiritual teachings comes the understanding we have four bodies:

1 — physical body
2 — mental body
3 — emotional body
4 — spiritual body

While, in truth, there are no separate bodies, delineating these categories is helpful for discussion since they describe unique states. As we explore these four main avenues of human expression, we learn to bring them into alignment with our divine nature; thus beginning a new adventure on earth — the spiritualization of matter.

# The Physical Body

When we look at our bodies, they appear to be solid like the world around us. We take our perception to be absolutely true. But is it? When scientists look at the cells of our bodies under a microscope, they do not see something solid. They see energy spinning around itself.

Deepak Chopra, a physician and spiritual teacher has keenly investigated the area of human perception and physical reality. He has come to the conclusion that perception is relative to the observer: that we literally create our physical reality based on our life experiences and the perceptions we form from these experiences. In his book *Ageless Body: Timeless Mind*[1], he discusses how this phenomenon affects the actual make-up of our bodies, their diseases and the process of aging. He demonstrates repeatedly how the mind/consciousness is the key factor in healing illness and maintaining youth.

Basically, Chopra postulates, there is a unifying consciousness which underlies the body and creates it in every moment. This core intelligence performs the body's mechanics; regulates its chemistry, cellular memory and growth. It is what makes us who we are and changes as we change. Therefore, physical reality is not fixed as we have thought, but open and fluid. Chopra feels we can work with inner awareness to release limiting beliefs and open to the greater possibilities of health and wholeness contained in our essence as cosmic consciousness.

When we were infants, we had a necessary interest in, and attachment to, our physical bodies; our focus was purely on survival. Also, those taking care of us directed their attention towards satisfying our physical needs.

In many ways, we, as a species have remained fixated at this primal place. Our identification of self has crystallized around the notion 'I am the body,' and our behaviors flow from this core belief. It is a hard notion to shake. If we believe we are only our physical bodies, then we will have to do everything in our power to preserve them; and we have. Unfortunately, this survival orientation has created much of the suffering on this planet.

The corollary to survival is death: non-survival. Overwhelming fear and anguish arise with this thought. We are imbued with the primal need to survive and will do whatever is necessary to protect ourselves. We have turned on each other vehemently to protect our land and our property whenever we felt threatened. We have been unbelievably aggressive toward others who stood in the way of our getting what we wanted or needed for our survival. This behavior has extended into religious wars as well as territorial disputes. People who looked or thought differently we have perceived as a threat to us, necessitating our need to kill or annihilate. Even at this date, one hears the motto of Western business, 'survival is the bottom line.' Somehow everything is justified if it comes from that place.

Individually, we have allowed ourselves to be treated in atrocious ways 'in order to survive.' We have remained in situations where we have been beaten and physically violated: we have tolerated emotional neglect and abuse. We thought we had no choice. We have given up our hearts and souls in the name of survival. Is that really all we came here to do — just survive? Surely there is more...

Perhaps, we can examine together the planetary paradigm of what is true for us. Perhaps we can open to the idea that what appears to us as solid and real is truly an illusion: a conglomeration of ideas, an agreed upon hypnotism that we accepted at birth. While this hypnotism has been a necessary part of our human experience, allowing us to experience the issues around separation, it is time to know the truth. Ramana Maharshi, the great Indian saint describes it so:

> *Take the instance of moving pictures on the screen in the cinema-show. What is there in front of you before the play begins? Merely the screen. On that screen you see the entire show, and for all appearances the pictures are real. but go and try to take hold of them. What do you take hold of? Merely the screen on which*

*the pictures appeared. After the play, when the pictures disappear, what remains? The screen again.*

*So with the Self. That alone exists, the pictures come and go. If you hold onto the Self, you will not be deceived by the appearance of the pictures...With the pictures the Self is in its manifest form: without the pictures it remains in the unmanifest form...It is quite immaterial if the Self is in one form or another. (One) is always the Self.*

— Be As You Are: The Teachings of
Sri Ramana Maharshi, *edited by David Godman*[2]

I do not wish to deny the value of the body as many religions have taught. The body is where this experience of consciousness is happening. It is a miraculous metaphor of cosmic intelligence. Within every cell is the stuff of the universe, not ever separate from itself. The body is the unique expression of the divine in form. It is holy. Sacred. And yet, we are so much more...

We are being asked now, at this point in history, to stretch our consciousness to hold a paradox. We are not **either** the body **or** the divine. We are both. The transformation of the species is at hand.

# The Mental Body

*The only way is to take full cognizance of the ways of one's mind and to turn it into an instrument of self-discovery. The mind was originally a tool in the struggle for biological survival. It had to learn the laws and ways of Nature in order to conquer it. That it did, and is doing, for mind and Nature working hand-in-hand can raise life to a higher level. But, in the process the mind acquired the art of symbolic thinking and communication, the art and skill of language. Words become important. Ideas and abstractions acquired an appearance of reality, the conceptual replaced the real, with the result that man now lives in a verbal world, crowded with words and dominated by words.*

*Obviously, for dealing with things and people words are exceedingly useful. But they make us live in a world totally symbolic and, therefore, unreal. To break out from this prison of the verbal mind into reality, one must be able to shift one's focus from the word to what it refers to, the thing itself.*

*— Maurice Fydman (Translator of Sri Nisargadatta Maharaj) — I Am That*[3]

The mental body, or 'mind,' refers to the thinking aspect of our being; the part that contains images, thought-forms and ideas that we identify with and act out in our daily lives. Pervading our awareness, the mind is always active, even during sleep. It defines who we are and what is real for us. Helping to solve problems, it is a powerful tool of consciousness.

The mind has a unique ability to be conscious of itself which is a breakthrough phenomenon in biological evolution. Yet, it is just this capacity that has caused it to become narrow, obsessive and repetitive.

It can latch onto ideas and ruminate incessantly creating a great energy drain in human psyches. Much of its attention has been focused around survival. We are talking here about the primitive aspect of the mind that creates fear and limits our experience, not the expansive, all-knowing mind that lies underneath.

Eastern mystical traditions have taught the necessity of stilling the mind in order to achieve enlightenment. We even hear it said, 'kill the mind.' Most of the world's saints and sages have seen the mental body as the greatest obstacle to spiritual development.

It is true in a way. The mind, or intellect, is the storehouse of the past. It contains our limiting thought forms and beliefs about reality. Then, it projects these images onto the future, based on past beliefs, telling us endlessly that we are in danger and must protect ourselves. It insists we can't trust others or ourselves: its underlying premise being, 'life is dangerous, and we are guilty, unworthy.' Its talk goes on and on — seemingly out of our control.

Perhaps we do not need to kill the mental body, but rather find a way to use this great instrument — instead of being used by it. Part of the process of claiming the mind is to see it for what it is: a succession of thoughts, images and ideas from the past, having no relevance to the present moment. It is out of space and time, coming from old experiences where we had limited understandings.

A way to begin to sort through all of this activity is to pay attention to the self-talk of the mind; not the story behind it, but the actual words and energies. Our thoughts have a repetitive/obsessive quality to them. They say the same things:

- 'I made a mistake. I'm so stupid.'
- 'I'm a failure, nothing I ever do is right, or good enough.'
- 'No one will ever love me, I'm unlovable.'
- 'Am I right or am I wrong? Is this good or is this bad?'

Over and over — ad nauseam.

In fact, one spiritual teacher talks about the dog eating his own vomit. That is us, picking up the same old stuff, eating it day after day — 'yummy...' — as if it actually tasted good, or could nourish us in some way.

We need to examine the contents of the mental body, impartially, and simply see what's there; not to criticize or analyze but just to look. We can do it alone, or with the help of a professional. Keeping a journal is helpful. What it really takes is a deep commitment to stopping all the drama and getting down to business. By ruthlessly investigating our thoughts, we begin to see what is false. Then the underlying truth can be readily seen.

Let your own investigation consist of being quiet and watching your mind, noticing what comes forward. It helps to observe your emotional reactions, moods and behaviors during the course of a day. By examining the thoughts underneath the feelings, you can then see what's really going on: thoughts trigger emotions.

The experience is humbling. It's like you're saying 'no more nonsense, let's just see what's in there,' without intellectualizing or making excuses. What you find can be quite amazing. There is nothing there of any value or truth! Most often we see the young child with its old hurts and mis-perceptions:

- 'Maybe he doesn't like me.'
- 'I'm not good enough.'
- 'It's my fault, I'm bad.'
  or
- 'It's not my fault, I'm not to blame.'

You may discover the mind engaged in rehearsal:

- 'What should I wear today to get a response from others?'
- 'What will I say if this, or that happens?'

We rehearse imaginary dialogues and scenarios based on imaginary ideas of ourselves and other people:

- 'If I do this, how will others react, and how will I feel about that?'
- 'I bet they're feeling this way and I don't agree — what's wrong with them or me?'
or
- 'What should I do about that — how do I respond, what should I say...?'

We are usually thinking about the future or the past, a behavior long recognized in esoteric philosophy. In fact, most religious and mystical practices have been designed to bring us into the present moment, away from the chattering mind that can only feed us past images. Drumming, dancing, singing, praying, fasting, chanting, meditating — all serve to distract or occupy the mind. It is felt we could be free if only we could become present. Our problems seem to arise from this troublesome mind!

How many of us have been around elderly people who are 'living in the past.' We know how tiresome that can be. The worst part is that we realize we are not seen by them as who we are now, but only as some ghostly echo from their past. It is the same with people who are mentally ill. They are tormented by events from their past that keep re-circulating in their minds, creating pain and misery.

And yet, we are all like that to some extent. We carry within us old hurts, rejections, and painful experiences from the past which don't allow us to live now, in the present moment. We see those around us as adversaries from whom to protect ourselves, even though our real adversaries may be dead and gone. We feel afraid though the present moment holds no danger. We constantly project onto others the faces from our past and then react accordingly. I remember Fritz Perls, the founder of Gestalt Therapy saying: 'Is this you I am meeting, or my projection of you?'

As we explore different aspects of the mental body, we become aware of how clever and creative the mind can be. This facility can be used in productive ways: writing, problem solving and spontaneous living. The problem is, the mind has been out of control for such a long time dictating our lives, that we simply accept it; it's like an old friend. Time to take charge!

One of my favorite pastimes is to watch the mind, like a cat sitting in front of a mouse hole. As long as the cat is watching, the mouse won't come out. It is the same with our thoughts. When we bring our awareness to them, simply as observers, the thoughts disappear or lessen in intensity. The power of our consciousness is so great that when awareness is present, what doesn't resonate with truth is revealed for what it is: not real.

We can choose where to focus our attention. In fact, that is the only real power we have when it comes to the mental body. Thus the old adage, 'It seems to have a mind of it's own.' We can learn to not grab onto the thoughts as they arise. By seeing they hold no truth for us, we don't choose to energize them. This is not repression, but actually choosing where we place our attention. Energetically where we put our attention is what we will experience. If we focus on pain, then our lives will be painful. If we focus on peace, our lives become peaceful. That is cosmic law. Our real power lies in our choices.

I choose to focus on the heart, a place where I can most directly feel the Self's true essence — pure love. By tracing thoughts energetically to their origin we find the peace and silence that sits underneath and gives rise to all experiences. There truly is nothing there but the divine. When we go deeper to this place, it's as if 'the game is up.' There's no need to suffer anymore. We are free.

The mental body itself seems to be asking for a rest, tired of all the endless dialogues and images. It wants to be used brilliantly, freshly and lovingly. As we stop the repetitive mind (the past), the pure, fresh, deeper mind can come forth in transcendent wisdom. When the gurus said 'get rid of the mind' this is what they meant. They were referring to the obsessive mind, not the silent exquisite intelligence that underlies it.

It is very rare to find people living in the moment. When we do, they often feel weird to us, as if they 'march to a different drummer.' They are paying attention to something other than old images and thoughtforms, and are attuned to the pulsations in and around them that open the way to rich experiences in every moment. This way of being is available to all of us. We must simply desire freedom more than anything. Being imprisoned by the mind doesn't work, it only creates suffering.

Being present is quite an amazing experience. Time stops, and we find ourselves in the ever present moment. Each moment is a new discovery. Events and ideas just unfold. Even the words out of our mouths flow effortlessly, totally appropriate to each situation. A sense of wonder replaces worry and depression. It's like when we were very young and lived totally in the magical moment. In the moment, anything can happen. Each event or idea is valued and experienced fully. The Inner Self is trusted totally: there is no separation. The frenzy slows down and there is the peaceful feeling of each moment being perfect: nothing is wrong. Everything is as it should be.

# Emotional Body

In my experience the emotional body is the most misunderstood part of us. It seems to act totally out of our control, creating great confusion, frustration and pain. Our logical thinking cannot touch or reason with it. Acting independently of our true wishes, it seems to have a life force of it's own. We used to say 'the devil made me do it,' and some religions still believe this.

Actual awareness of our emotional system has only opened up in the last one hundred years, with Freud describing an unconscious that governs ninety percent of our behavior. Up to that point, we didn't have a clue about how to understand and express our emotions. We felt powerless in their turbulence. They appeared to ebb and flow for no apparent reason, causing us to react with violence, depression, sadness or guilt. The only responses we saw around us were emotional outbursts, or feelings held in. We did not know we had other choices.

I see our emotional system as a technology that has taken a long time for us to understand. We now have tools and clarity we didn't have before. As we bring Western understanding of psychology and physics together with Eastern mysticism we can begin to understand a system that has long been our deepest pain but which can be our greatest joy.

The emotional body is an aspect of us, like our hands and feet, that has a specific function. It is made up of highly charged electrical energy which allows us to experience a phenomenon known as 'emotions.' This experience is little known or developed in other species. By being able to experience emotions, we can most closely know the actual energies of cosmic intelligence; love, joy, bliss, and peace, which are focused in the human heart. In a way, you might say our adventure here as humans is to experience the possibilities of ecstatic love in ways never known in the universe. The emotional body is our vehicle and expression for this possibility. Along the way, we have been experimenting with various intensities and frequencies of this electrical energy, often getting trapped or bogged down in its lower octaves of expression: pain, misery, and suffering. We have become lost, confused, and overwhelmed. It has seemed at times that we are foreigners in a strange land, unable to grasp the language and purpose of our human experience.

I find the emotional body to be the most primitive of our four bodies. It is the only one that hasn't grown 'one inch' since we first came upon this planet thousands and thousands of years ago. 'Fight or flight' is its operating principle. Imagine a primitive creature crawling out of the water for the first time and looking around; it would see limited resources, dangerous animals and a generally hostile environment. It might say to itself, 'This is a dangerous place. There is not enough food to go around. Now, what do I have to do to survive?' You can also imagine a young child saying the same things to itself as it looks around at its family. 'What do I need to do to survive here? Do I need to be good, smart or quiet? Do I need to try to take care of my parents? Do I need to control my feelings? Deny my needs?' This is where it happens. This is where we make the decisions around survival that stay with us throughout our lives. They influence our personality development (or lack of it) and all our relationships and life choices.

Our species has been developing over time. Our mental body has matured: we have become smarter; we know more. Our physical body has developed: we are healthier and live longer. Our spiritual body has expanded allowing us to have a glimmer of a higher, vaster existence. But our emotional body has not grown at all. This helps explain why people who are intelligent or wise can act in ways that are childish or dangerous: the guru misusing his power to gain wealth or sexual favors; the brilliant businessman being unable to talk to his wife or deal with his emotions; high-level government negotiations collapsing over ego or power issues. Jealousy and rage run rampant. We see attachment to self-image, or paranoid fantasies about people trying to hurt us. The list goes on and on with endless examples of emotional bodies out of control, playing havoc with themselves and each other.

Energetically, at this point in history, the emotional body has a very slow vibration. It is dense and heavy, affecting the way we feel. We often describe ourselves as feeling 'down,' 'heavy' or 'depressed.' We explain, 'I'm not myself today' as if we realize that something has taken over which is really not our true self. Emotionally this dense energy is felt as fear, unhappiness, despair, guilt, anger, sorrow, jealousy, frustration, powerlessness and hopelessness.

Developmentally, the emotional body is at a two year old level. It does not listen to reason: it wants what it wants when it wants it. If frustrated it goes into a tantrum. It is very attached to what it knows, what it is familiar with, so it doesn't like change. Try to give a clean blanket to a young child and it will refuse, clutching it's old, dirty blanket. It becomes attached to it's patterns of comfort very early in life.

An important aspect of the emotional body is it's tendency to become addicted to pain, misery and suffering. The heart of the emotional body is located in the solar-plexus area. We all know the feeling that grabs us in the stomach when we feel afraid, hurt, or angry. These feelings trigger the vagus nerve in the stomach, which sends a signal to the brain: 'Danger, danger! Do I need to run, hide, attack or withdraw?' In the brain, there is an electromagnetic stimulus — a 'pow' — a charge that goes through the body. The emotional body is addicted to this stimulation.

That's why behavior is so hard to change. We're not ignorant, we're just addicted. We're addicted to the adrenalin rush of fear, anger, and despair. There is a kind of excitement. Think about people seeing horror movies, or 'tear-jerkers.' We are addicted to the energies of fear or sadness. We are addicted to danger, to food, to relationships, to exercise, to working hard, to success, to failure, to depression, to abuse, to being a victim. The list goes on and on.

On the positive side it doesn't have to stay that way. The emotional body is now in a process of growth and evolution. The two year old is starting to grow up. With that change comes the possibility of experiencing the potential of this highly charged electrical system, the higher ranges of emotion: joy, rapture, ecstasy, love, peace, balance and harmony.

How can this happen? By introducing the energies of love and light into the places in the body where the emotional energy is crystallized, these slow energies can quicken their frequencies and move toward the light. All living systems move toward the light when given the chance: a plant stuck in the corner of a dark room will reach its tendrils toward the light. So, we don't have to fight with our emotional bodies, and we don't have to push them away. We can bring light into the body and allow this transmutation of energy to occur easily, naturally.

The growth process involves weaning the emotional body away from it's doses of anger, fear, and pain and giving it new tastes: the frequencies of love, joy and peace. These are much more delicious. If you dress the body in fine silk after it has been accustomed to rough wool, it may take a while to adjust to that softer, finer feeling. Eventually, it grows to love the new sensations.

We can begin to replace old destructive patterns and addictions with something much more nourishing and life enhancing.

# Experiencing the Divine

———⌘———

Ecstasy, bliss, joy, and love are our birthright. We come into life immersed in radiance and wholeness: our communion with Self is our only reality. As we develop unique identities, we move away from the rapture of divine union and our painful dance with separation begins.

But, these divine frequencies are not far away: they live in the Inner Child and can be recaptured instantly. The Higher Self, too, is there for the asking, 'in the twinkling of an eye.' We just have to remember...

# The Inner Child

Much has been said and written about the Inner Child. How-ever, most of the attention has been on the hurt, wounded child, or what I call the 'adapted child.'

There is another child, a natural child sitting inside us — pure, joyful, playful and wise. It is untouched and present now. It is eagerly waiting to be seen, acknowledged and expressed. Most of us are not in touch with this Inner Child because our emotional pain is so great. We turned away from this Essential Self at an early age deciding it was worthless, unimportant, and was not going to help us survive. Most often the reactions from those around us caused us to suppress our energies of exuberance, creativity, curiosity and imagination. We were told 'keep quiet' — 'behave' — 'don't talk back.' We were told we were crazy for talking to imaginary playmates, seeing elves or colors around people. Our intuitive perceptions were invalidated if they didn't match the hypnotism of the larger culture. Our feelings were silly or crazy if our parents didn't agree, since they too were in denial of their own Inner Child. We were admonished, 'it's only your imagination.' We, ourselves turned from this Inner Child, deciding it was unworthy, bad, a disappointment, 'not good enough.' If it was not valued by those around us, then we were not going to value it either.

Prevailing notions in education have supported the idea that the child is an empty vessel, primitive and ignorant, that we need to civi-lize and fill with knowledge. Methodologies of education have spo-ken about the necessity of 'breaking the child's will,' getting children to 'obey at all costs,' and they describe cruel ways of doing this. While we like to think this is in the past, these beliefs still resonate in our culture and in the cells of our bodies.

It is rare to grow up with an intact Inner Child. Some have kept the connection longer than others but, ultimately, we have succumbed to it's denial. As we moved into adulthood, we felt the aching loss of the joys and innocence of childhood. We have distant memories of the magic of living in the moment, the adventure of discovery, the creative play of the imagination. We remember the trust that all was well and the comfort that we were being taken care of. As we were in touch with the joys of nature and animals, so we also felt a passionate love for people. We experienced the openness, ecstasy and optimism of all things being possible.

The Inner Child is so important because it is the direct expression of the Higher Self in a physical body. It is the bridge from the spiritual into the physical, having a direct hotline to God. It carries forth the talents, gifts and wisdoms of this particular being. It knows us on a soul level and what we have come to share and experience in this life. It is the essence of who we are, our truest Self: divinity in form. It is always connected to that infinite vastness of possibilities, so its ways of self-expression are unlimited. The child comes into this world knowing how to love, knowing what it needs and knowing what it loves to do. It is in a way pre-programmed, like the seed of a flower.

The Inner Child is fearless: it knows there is no death, since it is connected to the womb of creation, the cosmic intelligence. The child comes in with its arms wide open, ready to love and be loved, eager to give its gift and excited about this great adventure. Most spiritual literature promises 'Be as the child and enter the kingdom of God.' So, how did we become so separated from our true inner joy? And how can we re-claim this divine child?

## GIFT EXCHANGE

It is not difficult. It is heart-near: we have but to call it in. Balance and knowing are the true nature of the Inner Child, as reflected in states of high energy, happiness and peace. If you call forth the Inner Child and it is not radiant and happy, then it is not in balance. Seeking this balance, a simple technique one can use is called 'The Gift Exchange.' You simply ask the child what gift it needs, from you, to come into balance and harmony: a color, symbol or object. Keep it simple. Give this gift and have the child take it **into** its body. Then see what happens: the child may ask for a Teddy Bear, then take the bear into its solar-plexus; as that softness radiates through its body, fear subsides, allowing the child to become happy, radiant.

Further, the child could give 'you' a gift for you to come into balance at this moment in your life. Take it into your body and see how it makes you feel. Are you relaxed, expansive, energetic, loved, happy? Lastly, embrace the child, feel it melt into you and allow it to permeate every cell of your body. You are re-uniting with your Divine Self, your Inner Child.

The reason we take the images into the body is that images actually carry energy. Thus we are translating experience from the mental to the physical realm. The body needs to 'feel' the safety of love, not just 'know it.' I find this to be the core of what is missing in current psycho-therapies: they don't allow for the clearing and movement of energy within the physical body.

If you do this exercise regularly, you will experience an inner transformation. You will realize that you are indeed an energy master, that you can 'tune the dial' to change emotions. Feelings, or states of being are not fixed. They are fluid and can be moved easily. The child can actually go from pain to happiness in a few minutes. And so can we: because the Inner Child is us.

The more we are united with our Inner Child, the more whole we will feel in our lives. The child really wants **us** to be there: to love, protect, and acknowledge it. When that attention doesn't happen, we try to fulfill our needs outside us: in lovers, children, food, alcohol or drugs. Is it not ourselves we are really searching for?

And it is so natural.

The more we practice merging with the Inner Child, the more we awaken feelings of ecstasy, the current of joy which is our birthright.

# Contacting the Higher Self

Simply invite it in. It has been waiting patiently for you to ask. The best way is just to sit quietly, take a few deep breaths and close your eyes. Feel your body begin to relax and let go of it's tensions. Do this for just a few minutes.

Now, ask your Higher Self to come forward. This is the tricky part. Here come our expectations of what it's supposed to look or feel like. What you want to do here is take the first thing that comes: a color, symbol, object, feeling or form. Wanting it to be something sensational — exploding fireworks or the 'old man on the mountain with a beard,' we try to disregard the easy, the familiar, such as the purple color we often see in meditation, or the peaceful feeling that fills us. The Higher Self can really be anything: a mountain, a kitten, a tingling sensation, a butterfly, a crystal, or an angel. The main idea here is to look for the nature of the 'energy' radiating from it. Is it soft, loving, warm, solid, light — protective, powerful or wise?

Then, feel that energy coming toward you, surrounding you. Let your body relax into it, embraced by this energy — enveloped in it's love, warmth and protection. Like being inside a cocoon.

At this point you might want to ask it for guidance or a gift to help you in your life now (like strength, courage, wisdom, etc...). Ask the Higher Self to put this into a symbolic form or color that you can then take into your body. It can enter anywhere. Feel the energy of that gift permeating your body.

Then, take the Higher Self into your body, filling you with it's radiance, love, power or whatever it is representing to you that day. Feel that energy flow through your body and instruct the cells to imprint it. This imprinting is important, as it begins to activate the cellular memory of your divine nature. It is coming home to the Self.

Note how this energy feels and what it creates inside you. Does your body seem to expand, feel tingly or warm? Is there a sense of wholeness, fullness, completeness? Do you feel loved? Is the energy fast? Slow? Fluid? Electric? You might call in physics terms to describe these fast moving energies.

**The Higher Self is energy** — it is the core energy of you, connected to every other energy. So, begin to be aware of it in your body as energy, not only as a mental idea; then it will become real to you. 'Spirit into matter' — that is the point. As you become acquainted with this energy, this presence, it will become like an old friend. It may come in differently every day, or stay the same. It doesn't matter.

It is important to know that the Higher Self is connected to the Self in all it's totality. So, when you ask for help, remember it can flow in from any direction. The bird singing in the tree outside your window reminding you of joy; the old woman saying to you on your morning run 'stay with it' just when you were feeling discouraged; a character on television telling her sister how to assert herself with her husband at a time when you were struggling with the same issue. In the Indian tribes, the elders ask: 'What are the children saying, Which way are the birds flying?'

We are not alone, not an isolated Self. We are the Self that looks back at us in all the faces we see, in the substance of everything that is. That's why it is so limiting for people to say 'I won't ask for help, I should be able to handle this myself.' The Self is **everywhere**, ready to help us. We only have to ask. We only have to 'see,' and be open.

In my own experience, I find that the form the Higher Self comes in often represents a teaching for me. It once came to me as a powerful tree, rooted in the ground with it's branches raised to the sky. It was reminding me to stay grounded as I reached for the stars. Another time it came to me as Buggs Bunny, laughing hysterically at me for being so serious. The message that came was, 'lighten up kid.'

While the Higher Self sometimes has a sense of humor, I find it can also be dead serious, screaming at me to 'wake up.' It may speak in words, though I have found words or messages to be somewhat unreliable. The emotional body can move in quickly with it's own needs, creating an 'infiltrate,' telling me what I want to hear.

Mostly, I just pay attention to the energy, open to it, and merge with it. It has become an underlying hum of ecstasy that is always with me. As it fills me, I'm aware of it moving me — talking me, inspiring me. I have a growing sense of not being the 'doer' anymore. Life bursts forth from a vast joyful place that I cannot understand, but can witness and allow. Ideas come to me as I need them. Knowing what to say flows from my lips more beautifully and clearly than I have ever experienced. Life's circumstances are orchestrated perfectly for me to awaken. Help is always there in some form: a friend, a book, a knowing.

As you begin to work with your Higher Self, you will start to notice the difference in frequencies and learn to attune to only those energies that create joy, love, power and light. You will become like a tuning fork, feeling the difference between fast and slow frequencies. Then, you will be on your way to becoming an energy master, claiming your birthright of divine radiance.

# It Takes Practice

Any new skill requires practice. We didn't learn to ride a bicycle the first time we tried. Learning to tune into our Higher Self is the same thing. We have to practice. We are learning to exercise a special muscle that we haven't used very much. Some of us didn't even know it was there.

It is a good idea to stop several times a day, and check inside. Just see what's there. Get to know your Higher Self, as your most intimate friend. Put the same energy into this relationship as you would a fascinating new lover or a precious newborn baby. Let it kiss you, embrace you. See what that feels like. Get to know it's rhythms, desires and passions. When it comes close, does it have a fragrance or melody? When you touch it, does it send a quiver through your body?

How much time and energy have we spent in thinking about a new lover? We obsess about what we will wear, what we will say. We dream about all the pleasure that will come to us at our meeting. We create fascinating scenarios; we write love songs and poetry. We are breathless in anticipation of this great experience of lovemaking: ecstasy, merging with our beloved.

Now, we can have this experience every moment. Each time we stop to be with our Higher Self, we are merging with our true beloved. At it's touch, come all the possibilities of divine expression. Peace can fill us in the midst of turmoil. Love finds it's way to our hearts when we are being critical. Answers come to our questions instantaneously or later, as an intuitive flash.

**We have only to ask.** All spiritual literature tells us this. The vast intelligence will not interfere: we have to invite it in. That is part of what we're doing here on this planet, choosing to become conscious.

Ask the Higher Self for clarity around any area with which you are dealing: personal struggles, relationships, occupational or economic issues. Nothing is too mundane. You can ask it what to eat, how to dress, or whether to go to the movies. Then, pay attention to the feelings, images or ideas that come to you.

Everything is holy. We have become so accustomed to pushing away the Self, that we ignore and distrust much of what comes to us from the inner levels. It is a very old habit. We call our knowings silly, unimportant or 'only our imagination.' Often, people recall times when their first instinct about a person or event turned out to be correct, but they didn't trust themselves. The truth is so close, so real: it whispers to us continually. Our only job is to stop, listen and trust. It is here now. We don't have to go anywhere or do anything.

You can call the Higher Self in directly and see how it comes to you, relating to it as a form or energy. You can also just tune into the silence in your heart, or the 'detached observer.' It may express as an underlying current or sound. You may discover a favorite way to attune with your divine presence. Some prefer to think in traditional forms, such as Christ or Buddha. Just remember, what is important is the energy of these forms, not the form itself. People who respond more to nature feel better with natural images such as wind, water, mountains or animals. Scientific-minded people prefer physical energies like light, sound, electrical current or radiance.

What matters is that it be something personal to you that you can identify easily. Many people relate how familiar the Higher Self is to them in some very profound way, like a forgotten voice of the past which has always been there, has never gone away. It was the undercurrent of their lives, while they were off doing something else. It is so natural after all.

What is so helpful about conceptualizing the spiritual presence into symbolic form, is that a bridge is created from our concrete reality into the unknown. What the brain can see, touch or feel, will register as real. This also is a powerful way to begin to get acquainted with the ecstatic frequencies a little at a time, so the body can become familiar with them: like putting your toe into the water and taking it out again. Then putting it in again for a longer period, until you are comfortable with the water temperature. Since the whole process is guided by divine intelligence, you will go at the rate that is most harmonious for you. You will feel a sense of control that is helpful as you approach this vast mysterious presence. Then, experiencing happiness, peace and love doesn't have to be 'happenstance.' You can simply 'tune the dial' to access and live in these magnificent frequencies.

You may prefer to just be with the silence within and to completely let go of any mental concepts, going beneath the physical senses, the intellect, the emotions, and staying in the 'everpresent stillness.' Deepening into that place, you will experience the richness and fullness of divine energies, and be nourished in a most profound way. The depth just grows. You may still ask for guidance, but the response may not be so linear. Perhaps the feeling of wholeness is enough to release the sense of inadequacy or fear. Feelings and intuitions may become the 'answers.' This practice involves the development of great sensitivity within.

Taking a longer time to meditate is also very important, along with checking inside periodically throughout the day. This attention allows for a deepening of the inner connection and makes these energies more real to us. Otherwise, the 'mesmerism' of the world can take over very rapidly. It takes a strong desire to develop new habits and re-focus our attention.

*Part Two*

# Multi-Incarnational Exploration

# The Theater of the Soul

———————— ∞ ————————

*'All the world's a stage*
*And all the men and women merely players.*
*They have their exits and their entrances;*
*And one man in his time plays many parts...'*
— *William Shakespeare*
As You Like It

How can we comprehend our existence here? How do we make sense of it? Playwrights, poets, philosophers and theologians have contemplated these mysteries from the beginning of time. William Shakespeare was a great visionary who had the rare capacity to step back and see truth from an expanded perspective. He understood so well that human experience is centered around our comedies, tragedies, and triumphs, which he explored with humor and compassion. Many, like myself, have come to the same conclusion, that our purpose here is related to the stories we have created on a soul level in order to have a particular kind of experience.

In reincarnational theory, belief is centered around the continuity of a soul that takes on different bodies in successive lifetimes to work out its karma. The inner being is the focus not the external body it happens to be wearing at the time. We put on bodies, like clothing, and take them off when we are finished with them. The time period is considered illusory, not a true reality but only the setting or backdrop for the experience the soul is having.

'The play's the thing.' It certainly seems that way. We as a species put on costumes, play roles and carry on in the most outrageous ways; sometimes a comedy, sometimes a tragedy. The daily stuff of our lives is acting, playing out our stories. We are totally fascinated with the movies, plays, novels, operas — all the theater arts. Our conversations with each other are centered around 'who said what to whom.' Dialogue, characters, setting, mood, costumes, dramatic tension, comic relief. Is there anything else we're concerned about?

From my perspective as a psychotherapist, the most effective therapies involve playing out our life stories in a dramatic way. Multi-Incarnational Therapy is particularly successful in doing this since it provides a comfortable and safe environment for scenarios to be experienced. Stories flow easily and naturally from our innate ability to see life in this way. We are all born actors... In the process, whatever has been blocking our sense of well-being, joy and aliveness can be seen and released.

I believe the main purpose of therapy is to bring into awareness those emotional patterns that have been hidden from us and creating difficulty in our lives. When we are conscious of these patterns, the light of truth can dissolve them. After the false is removed, truth is standing there; you don't need to search for it.

In this work, not only do we see the contents of our dramas, but we learn to tune into the Higher Self and to use that connection throughout the sessions. This connection is a powerful and profound experience. For most of us, it is the first time we have felt a direct communication with our Divine Self, and we are deeply moved. After a series of sessions we acquire an ease, a familiarity in tuning into the inner wisdom. For the first time, we learn to trust this powerful presence that has been orchestrating our sessions and our lives so exquisitely.

So, multi-incarnational exploration as a healing tool is particularly effective: it goes deep, works fast and brings compassion in the most beautiful way. The sessions are interesting, profound and fun, all at the same time. The soul's history is revealed in all its foibles, antics, tragedies and triumphs. What a play!

# Reincarnation

———————————⚭———————————

I remember at the age of eighteen being told about reincarnation, the philosophy of having previous lifetimes. At that time, I was an agnostic, but I accepted multiple lives as true. It just made sense deep inside. 'Of course.' I then tucked that idea away and didn't think about it again for twenty-five years, when I was introduced to multi-incarnational work as a healing tool.

Reincarnation makes sense to a lot of people. It is one of the main tenets of Hinduism along with the notion of karma. Karma is the result of actions taken in past-lives that we carry from lifetime to lifetime. Hindus see karma as unshakable and therefore totally accept their life circumstances without trying to change them.

Like me, many people who are not Hindus accept the concept of reincarnation simply because it 'feels right.' This is particularly true for children. Some children will even relate their previous lifetimes in a very matter-of-fact way. 'Are we going to die in a fire like we did before daddy?' or 'I love you both, mommy and daddy but when can I see the parents I had before?' Children often talk easily of these experiences if they are not made to feel badly about them. Sometimes the parents are too frightened to hear.

The concept of reincarnation or the continuity of the soul, can be found in most of the religions of the world. It was even present in Christianity before the eleventh century. Often reincarnation has been accompanied by a kind of fatalism or passivity which is difficult for the Western mind. We like the idea of being able to do something about our problems, to take action. We don't like the notion of being stuck in our lives, powerless to change. It is not the American way.

So Western religions have been formulated to include change and to emphasize the value of this life. 'This is all we have, so let's make the best of it.' Not a bad attitude, certainly more hopeful than accepting your suffering because it is your 'karma.'

In Multi-Incarnational Therapy, East and West are joined. The continuity of the soul is accepted and incorporated into the understanding of our multi-dimensional nature. However there is great fluidity and possibility for change, not just within this lifetime, but from moment to moment.

Essentially, karma is not fixed in stone, it is possible to be released instantly when one becomes aware of truth. Our dramas are not here to punish us but to serve as cosmic teaching tools, to understand the laws of energy — 'You sow what you reap' — 'You create your reality.' Things in nature need to be balanced. In linear time there is cause and effect. No punishing God, no jury. It is only our judgment that we carry from lifetime to lifetime; and that can be released.

# What is Multi-Incarnational Therapy?

The memory of the past unfulfilled desires traps energy, which manifests itself as a person. When its
charge gets exhausted, the person dies. Unfulfilled desires are carried over into the next birth. Self-identifi-
cation with the body creates ever fresh desires and
there is no  end to them, unless this mechanism of
bondage is clearly seen. It is clarity that is liberating,
for you cannot abandon desire, unless its causes and
effects are clearly seen. I do not say that the same person is reborn. It dies and dies for good. But its memories remain and their desires and fears. They supply
the energy for a new person. The real takes no part in
it, but makes it possible by giving it the light.

—*Sri Nisargadatta Maharaj*
I Am That

Multi-Incarnational Therapy is a method of exploring the past-
lives, stories and dramas that live inside us. Some people see it
as a way of investigating the archetypes of our collective unconscious.
It doesn't really matter how you see it, it works.

My own feeling, after doing this kind of work for ten years, is that
these lifetimes are real but not necessarily personal to us. When we
are born, we pick up strands of genetic material, a combination of
both parents, that holds a particular kind of emotional history. This

genetic pre-disposition determines the themes and issues that will emerge for us to learn and explore in this life. By entering past-lives, we experience the original time period where emotional patterns became established, allowing awareness to flow in with its light. Then, like a wave that ripples out, the resultant clearing affects those same issues in our lives now.

'Hear oh Israel, the Lord our God, the Lord is One.' If we come from a premise that there is really one cosmic intelligence having all these experiences, we can plug into any human experience that holds the potential for growth and understanding, and receive the benefit. So, from my perspective, the lifetimes are real but not necessarily personal, since there are no 'separate' selves in the larger scheme of things.

Here enters the Higher Self. It is the job of the Higher Self to select the lifetimes or experiences that will be of most benefit to that person's life now. The Higher Self knows us intimately. It knows just what we're ready for and the best way to go about getting it. If the person is fragile it will go slowly, showing them only scenarios where there was peace and harmony. If there is a readiness to go deeper, other issues may come forward revealing tendencies of control, misuse of power, or guilt.

Each person has a direct experience guided by a facilitator. The person does it. No one else really knows what we need but our own Higher Self. We trust that totally and sessions marvelously reflect that perfection. I am in a state of awe as I watch the Higher Self revealing each experience in so many powerful and original ways. Doing this work has profoundly deepened my trust and connection as a facilitator. I may think I know what the client needs, or where the session has to go, but the Higher Self continues to surprise me. I basically see my job as paying attention, staying tuned-in, and using my skills as a co-creator with this divine intelligence.

Day after day, as the lifetimes (or stories) are seen and released, the client begins to form a sense of a personal hologram, or soul's history. Feelings, problems and events from this lifetime begin to take on different meanings, to 'fall in place.' The perspective expands concerning why things happen, like stepping back and seeing the bigger picture. And so benevolent. No matter what happened — what pain or violence — the Higher Self always helps the person to forgive self and others through its infinite compassion.

# How It Works

Feelings are energy. Thought forms are energy. Scientists are coming to the same conclusion. When you take matter down to it's smallest particle, it is pure energy.

So, for any therapy to be effective it has to deal with the energetic level. It has been said that 'understanding is the booby prize.' Real change and transformation have to go deeper, to the subtle energy levels from which all things arise. Multi-Incarnational Therapy does that and also includes the mental realm of understanding that we humans seem to crave. In practice, multi-incarnational exploration is all inclusive, allowing all the four bodies to work together; physical, mental, emotional and spiritual, while recognizing they come from the same underlying energetic source.

Behavior patterns, thought forms, belief systems, emotions — all sit as crystallized energy in the cells of our bodies, a kind of cellular memory. Most of that is unconscious, out of our awareness but affecting our lives nonetheless. If these patterns were conscious we could do something about them, but unfortunately they are not. Therein lies the problem. The beauty of this work is that it allows for these trapped energies to become conscious so they can then be cleared. It's a way in.

In my experience, when some event or emotion can be directly felt, it is free to dissolve. The reason conflicts stay inside us unresolved is because the feelings were not truly experienced at the time they occurred or because the experience was misunderstood and judged. When these trapped energies can be brought forth into the light of day, they can be seen for what they are and released. In our history, we have simply been human beings doing the best we knew during times when the planet was ignorant of truth. We were not evil, as we often condemned ourselves for being. We **do** have a more developed awareness now, and this can be used to bring in forgiveness and understanding as we re-experience these old scenarios.

## THE DRAMA OF JUDGMENT

I find that healing is primarily a matter of releasing judgment. Judgment is truly the biggest problem humankind has had to face in the last several thousand years. Our polarity brains have only been able to think in terms of opposites: either/or, right/wrong, black/white, male/female. We have blamed and punished each other and ourselves. Only relatively recently has there developed a physical bridge between the right and left hemispheres of the brain, allowing for the merging of opposites and a flow of compassion. We have simply been trapped in our biology and our history.

All of us have participated in this play of consciousness. We have been the saint/sinner, tyrant/slave, victim/victimizer, teacher/student, barbarian/saint. We have all done everything. That understanding is a basic premise of this work. It is important to own this fact, to own all the different aspects of our human nature and to stop blaming others for our problems. 'Not me, I'm a good guy.'

We are all good guys basically. In fact, all that's inside us is light. In the movie *Cocoon* when the aliens zipped off their human bodies, there was only light. As are we. We have simply taken on various costumes and bodies to have particular experiences. In truth, nobody has been judging us but ourselves, and that misperception is what we're here to clear.

Judgment is vicious. It tells us we are evil, bad, unworthy — that we don't deserve to live, love or have what we want. It has separated us from our own hearts and turned us away from the only force that could give us love, peace and wisdom. Religious and political leaders who wielded power knew the laws of energy: you can control a person who is not centered in his own truth, her own heart. So these leaders made it their priority to cut people off from their essential nature. This drama exemplifies our planetary history, and we have literally participated in all sides of it.

In the process of all this activity, we have learned and grown as a species. We may now be ready to throw off this mantle of ignorance and claim our birthright as spiritual beings: to know that no one outside ourselves holds our truth; to know that truth is inside us as the Self. It is the benevolent shining presence that has never judged us, only loved us, **enough** to let us have our experiences and learn from them. It was always holding the light when we were ready for it, whenever we cried out for 'Help!' Not always in the form we wanted, but there nonetheless.

## DIRECT EXPERIENCE

In Multi-Incarnational Therapy, we have the opportunity to play out our 'unspeakables' in a way that is safe and somewhat detached, like watching a movie. We can play roles and have experiences currently unavailable to us. We can also witness possible outcomes of our current behavior patterns.

Most importantly, we have a direct experience. It has been scientifically demonstrated that when the mind images something, the message to the brain is: 'This experience is real' and acts accordingly. So in seeing ourselves in these various scenarios, we can 'experience out' whatever has been suppressed, coming into a place of balance, understanding and forgiveness. We can literally return to the past and heal it.

One of the criticisms of this kind of work is that it focuses on the past. I hear people say, 'I have enough problems in my present life, why go into the past?' But this view is short-sighted. It is coming from a belief locked into a linear view of reality: past, present, future. In truth all time is happening now, just in different dimensions, and these dimensions are interacting with each other continuously. That is why when you clear a fear of traveling that happened as a result of some trauma in fourteenth century Europe, it energetically removes the fear of flying in 1994 America. It is fascinating how this works.

We can even clear current relationships this way. I remember working with an American woman who had been living in Paris for twenty years. She had left her home in Chicago to become a model and live a Bohemian life abroad. Her father, a wealthy industrialist, had disowned her and they had not had any contact for twenty years.

Their estrangement was very painful to her, so she asked for sessions to clear her relationship with him. A letter from her father arrived ten days after the sessions, stating he wanted to have her back in his life, he missed her very much. The letter was dated the same afternoon she had cleared him in the session in Paris. They met in Chicago the following summer and there has since been an enormous healing. When we unravel the source of our energetic patterns, they are free to change in our lives now. Magic can happen.

If you don't believe in past lives, you can simply view this method as an effective way to get to the heart of a problem and clear it out. We are all connected as a species, with a collective unconscious or collective memory, according to Carl Jung. Within the cells of our bodies lies the entire history of the species; everything we have ever done, felt and experienced. This memory can be tapped into and utilized for growth and healing. Sometimes I am at a loss to explain how it works. It just does. You are free to explain the process in any way that works for you; past-lives, teaching stories, primal archetypes or creative visualizations.

## COMPASSION

Seeing oneself playing a personality that one is ordinarily disconnected from can bring great understanding and compassion. I could never understand the macho men who hang around the Plaza in Santa Fe where I live, calling out profanities to women. I used to view them as disgusting and alien to me. Then I had a lifetime where I was a macho male in Spain in the 1500's. I was able to experience the sadness and pain that comes from having to shut off feelings at an early age in order to be accepted as a male in Spanish culture. The need to fit in and be approved of was strong in those times. I saw how one can become cold and de-personalize others when one is shut off from his own feelings. After that, after I had 'walked in his shoes,' I felt more compassion for these men. Needless to say, they stopped bothering me. It tends to work that way. What is unfinished in us carries a charge of energy which sends out a signal for others to play out. When we claim and heal these patterns, we are free to draw in other kinds of behaviors. We are indeed the movie projector playing out our dramas on the screen of life. When we change the movie in the projector, there are different images played out on the screen.

I had a client once, a large heavy man with a big red bushy beard, a Paul Bunyan type. He was having marital problems that seemed insoluble. He and his wife had been working on their problems for several years and since there was no progress, she was getting ready to leave him. In his first session, he had a lifetime as a woman. He immersed himself so deeply into the experience that he could feel her breasts, her sexual organs, her softness, sensitivity and sensuality. Later, his wife reported that he could understand her for the first time in their marriage and was much more sensitive to her needs. Magic.

Both men and women have claimed their power after seeing themselves misusing it in other lifetimes. They discovered it was themselves they were afraid of. The capacity to speak one's truth and wisdom has emerged after lifetimes where the person was burned at the stake or ostracized from society for expressing themselves.

I have generally found it isn't the physical trauma that hurts us the most; it's the feelings unexpressed or the erroneous conclusions drawn that stay with us as unfinished business.

- 'Speaking out is dangerous.'
- 'I can't be trusted,' or, 'Others can't be trusted.'
- 'If you live from your heart, you will die.'

We simply haven't understood how the emotional body functions. We have either acted out our suffering through aggression and violence or have held our feelings in, creating disease and emotional deadness. We have not realized that feelings are energy, that they really only need to be experienced. We won't die. We simply have to breathe **into** emotions and they will fade. Pain is not endless but we can make it endure, by not feeling it, holding onto or resisting it. Watch small children when they feel strong emotions; the energy runs through them in a few minutes, and they are back to joy. Joy is our true nature.

We have so misunderstood emotions, we have wreaked havoc on our personal lives. If, as children, we felt afraid, angry or sad, we were told to keep quiet, not to express our feelings. If we did express, we were made to feel that we were selfish, disrespectful and unloving. We watched the adults around us holding everything in, denying their pain; or being abusive, depressed and numb. These responses became our models for how to handle emotions.

We've had a heavy history, but we are now in a position to change that. It is possible to feel the whole rainbow of human emotions effortlessly and naturally. It is our birthright. We can choose those feelings we wish to express or act out according to our inner wisdom, the pulsation of life. We can claim the joy and vitality that lives under pain and hurt. We can be fully alive and human in a new manner; not in a way that suppresses our feelings, but in a way that celebrates all of who we are!

# Who Is It For?

Multi-Incarnational Therapy is really for anyone. It is not diffi-cult. It is the most natural thing in the world to create stories. We do it as children, acting out our fantasies, our dreams. We love to play cowboys and indians, changing roles from day to day; we enjoy the fun of new and different adventures.

We are natural storytellers. We love the movies. In the book *Illusions* by Richard Bach the main character asked, 'What is the mean-ing of life?.' He was then taken to the movie theater for his answer. When he didn't understand, he was taken to another movie.

I find this work particularly appealing to men, since it has a sense of action and adventure. Women enjoy this method as it en-ables them to use and validate their natural tendencies to go within. We don't have to be good visualizers. We perceive in many ways other than by seeing: we can sense or feel the story; we can 'hear' it or even 'make it up in our minds.' In any case, we don't make up things we haven't experienced. It all works through using what is the best for you. The facilitator's job is to help you find and trust the way the lifetime comes to you.

**Trust**, in fact, is a big bonus of these sessions. We have such a tendency to discredit our own productions. 'Wasn't good enough' — 'silly or stupid' — 'only my imagination' — 'doesn't make any sense' or 'boring.' We have not had much encouragement in valuing our inner lives. As children we were punished for daydreaming. If our drawings were not of this reality, we were told they weren't any good. If we described our visions, dreams, or out-of-body experiences, we were quickly told not to talk about that to anyone. The message was clear. 'That is not a valid place to go, or talk about. Close it down.' And we have.

So in these sessions we learn to trust and value what comes out of us as the unique expression of the inner wisdom. For many people, this is the most healing thing that happens.

While everyone can do this work, there are certain ways to tell if the time is right. First, does this work appeal to you? Does it sound interesting or exciting? There is a kind of readiness factor: we are at a point in our lives where we want to go deeper into ourselves and to clear out what's in the way of being all we can be; we want to experience the joy and peace we know is possible and to give our gifts. Basically, we are ready to change our lives. Our dramas have become repetitive and uninteresting.

Often, people come who have been working on themselves for many years, psychologically or spiritually. They are at an impasse in their lives where things aren't moving. They may have great wisdom intellectually but their behavior hasn't changed in everyday life. They need help in going deeper into the energetic roots of their patterns. Some people come to this method as beginners. They haven't done much therapy or been on a spiritual quest. It is 'just time.' It can work equally well, perhaps better, because they don't have the so-called 'knowledge' to get past.

A basic requirement of this work is the readiness to take responsibility for our lives. To acknowledge that the source of our problems lies within ourselves, not in the outside world. We see this not from a place of self blame, but from understanding cosmic principles of energy. I tell clients, 'We don't do blame here.' If a person wants to continue to project onto others the source of their pain, then this work is not for them. We truly do create our own reality. The more we can claim that, the more we can claim the power.

I believe that our dramas and life themes are purposeful. We created them on a soul level to experience growth and understanding. We do not live in a random universe without meaning: every event is orchestrated to create a state of growth, to wake us up to who we really are, to allow us to give our gifts as unique expressions of cosmic intelligence.

It all makes sense when seen from this perspective:

- The woman who was victimized by her father in this life, may have been victimizing others in earlier lifetimes. The lesson:

learning about power and it's misuse.

- The woman, terrified of travel, learns of a lifetime where she travelled by boat with her mother, and everyone was killed but her. The pain of her abandonment has haunted her in this life and crippled her venturing out in the world.
- The businessman, unable to access his feeling, tender side, finds out that his past life as a woman held abuse and oppression. Vulnerability came to be considered weak and dangerous.
- The woman, desiring to express her artistic nature, discovers a lifetime where she was an obsessive artist, and nothing else mattered. Dying in that life of alcoholism and loneliness, she has a fear in this life that if she gives in to this artistic passion, she will be lost and alone again.

When such scenarios are seen, felt and released, the fears usually fade away, and we are ready to reclaim the part of ourselves we have disowned. The past is cleared allowing us to be more present in this life now. It works.

Multi-Incarnational Therapy is also for people who feel that something is missing in their lives. We yearn for connection to our deeper selves. In the process of living a busy goal oriented life, there is often a vague sense of emptiness inside, an ache in our hearts, a disconnection. This can be felt as a general malaise, reflected in eating or drinking too much, working too hard, watching too much television, or just feeling an underlying anxiety with no apparent cause. We may feel restless, depressed, irritable or sad.

Many people believe that the current problems limiting the world have to do with our being in a spiritual crisis. We have lost touch with our soul. Structured religions have become outmoded for a lot of us and nothing has replaced them. The search for inner meaning has taken many of us to Eastern mysticism and esoteric philosophy, but these often end up being intellectual exercises that still don't help us to know ourselves and to feel connected, day to day.

Innovative businesses are opening to the need to re-connect to our Inner Self. They are bringing poets into their companies to help people touch into their hearts. They are conducting seminars in communication and stress reduction. Leaders are recognizing that unhappy people make poor employees. If employees are tapped into their source, they are happier, healthier, more creative and productive human beings. Everyone benefits. **That** is the bottom line.

One of my first clients was a woman who worked in the U.S. State Department. Her job was to negotiate with leaders in Africa. She recounted a story where all the officials were sitting around the bargaining table at an impasse. Neither side would budge from its position. Out of desperation, she put in an inner call of 'help' to her Higher Self. Within minutes, words started to flow from her mouth that brought forth a wisdom and clarity that was very much needed. The tone of the meeting was entirely changed and things started to move.

This experience was a powerful imprint for me to begin to see this work as a tremendous catalyst for global harmony as well as individual peace. We don't always see the bigger picture, but there **is** an intelligence that does.

# How It Differs From Other Therapies

We are in the Jet Age, a time of space exploration, instantaneous communication and movements toward global cooperation. We are beginning to realize we are more than our own little worlds and our current dramas. There is a feeling of expansion into the greater possibilities of who we are, as individuals and as a species. Science is revealing the variability of time and ways our perception affects reality. Star Trek goes where no one has gone before.

This expanded thinking and excitement is reflected in our personal exploration. We sense that we are much more than our old paradigms have told us, that everything and everybody is connected in some very basic way. Time is an illusion: matter is energy: all time is simultaneous. There are other dimensions, other realities, beyond and including linear time and third dimensional reality. We are ready for philosophies, methodologies, and tools that can assist us in this 'speeding up,' that can bridge the past and present.

Essentially we need a therapy that can take all of this into consideration, that can combine the truth of science and the wisdom of spirituality, that values ancient mythology and modern psychology equally as valuable teaching tools. Opposites coming together. Paradigms shifting. Not 'either/or' but 'yes/yes.'

Multi-Incarnational Therapy sees the individual as part of a hologram, a matrix of energy that is all-inclusive, an essence that has been participating in all of earth's history and beyond. It understands we are not separate or limited, and certainly not powerless. This approach allows for exploration of countless dimensions and time periods, of different bodies and personalities. It can open the channel to guides, angels, colors, energetic states, galactic experiences, inner journeys and outer journeys. Everything is possible. It takes into account the understanding that we are multi-level creatures and all of our experiences interweave to create the uniqueness that we are.

Best of all, our Higher Self is in charge, guiding us to and through every experience with wisdom, grace and love. The partnership with the Higher Self is really what sets this work apart from other past-life therapies. The premise that we are spiritual beings underlies this work. We are not really interested in the form the Higher Self takes, we are more interested in what is meaningful for the individual person: be it a Christ being or a particle of light. The connection to this Self, practicing and deepening into it, creates a trust that was previously not there in the person's life. In addition, valuable tools are given throughout the sessions to help maintain that connection.

As a result, this form of therapy does not encourage dependency on the facilitator. Quite the contrary. Clients are encouraged from the beginning to 'ask your Higher Self' when anything comes up. That is really the purpose of this work: to facilitate the person getting in touch with, trusting and using the Higher Self in daily life. We simply help remove the blocks.

A motto of mine: 'It is important to plant flowers in a garden, as well as pull the weeds.' Both are essential. Not only is it necessary to look at conflicts and blocks, it is also vital to have experiences that lift us into the frequencies of love, joy, ecstasy, peace and power. It's a basic psychological principle that you don't remove something without replacing it. Everybody wins, especially the emotional body fed in a new way which can now evolve to match growth in other aspects of our being.

Throughout the sessions, we are bathed in love, support and wisdom. We learn to recognize these frequencies as 'home' and to become familiar with the presence underlying, calling it in as needed. The divine partnership is established, not as foreign or happenstance, but there as a continuous current, totally available every moment.

It **is** a new time...

# The Power of Love

**Love**, is essentially the baseline of this work. We put into practice the basic teachings of Christ and other great spiritual masters. Forgiveness is the key. We find that love and forgiveness are what heal our bodies, our relationships and our spiritual separation. When we enter the time period where the guilt, sorrow or anger became imprinted, we see with new eyes. We see that the character was not bad, perhaps a little misguided. The fact is we were just ignorant of truth. We did the best we could based on the circumstances of the times.

When we felt powerless, we went into a rage and tried to blame ourselves, others, or God. Sometimes all three. For example, if a child died in thirteenth century Europe. . .

- The mother blamed herself. She should have watched the child more closely.
- The father blamed himself. He was supposed to protect his family from harm.
- They both blamed the physician/healer, who didn't do enough to save the child.
  Or, the final blow:
- They blamed God — 'How could he take an innocent child?'

In many parts of the world, we are still caught in this way of thinking and response to life.

What then might happen in the above scenario: neither parent feels their grief and the pain of their loss. These feelings stay inside their bodies, unexpressed perhaps creating high blood pressure or a tumor that will later kill them. Instead of growing closer with their grief, they grow apart. The father eventually becomes an alcoholic to deaden his pain, and the mother lives out her life in depression and loneliness. Both die, carrying their pain, grief and guilt.

When we re-experience scenarios like this, we can bring to them a more enlightened consciousness. In truth, no one was to blame. Things just happen, that's life. We need to feel our pain and move on. Forgiveness and love can then pour forth automatically. There was nothing wrong. Souls make choices (in this case, the child) that we don't always have a way of understanding.

Even activities we consider pretty horrible, can make sense in the context of the time in which they occurred. The barbarian who serves his tribe by chopping off enemy heads is just doing his job: he is not evil. He has a wife, children, and is considered a hero, respected by his people. However, as he kills his one hundredth person, he may look into their eyes and feel something for the first time. He realizes what he has done. He has taken a human life, and the rest of his life is haunted with guilt and the eyes of everyone he has killed. He concludes at the end of the life: 'I'm a monster. I don't deserve love or happiness. I deserve to be punished.' Perhaps in the next life, he is a slave in Egypt whipped mercilessly. He wonders why God could be so cruel to him. It wasn't God punishing him, it was his own guilt that created this scenario.

This is how karma works. Karma is the principle of balance in the universe, continually moving towards harmony. Judgment puts our emotional system out of balance while forgiveness, love and compassion restore it. When forgiveness flows in, karma is instantly released. There is no need to play it out anymore.

We are not accustomed to responding to ourselves and life from a place of love. We are so quick to judge. Judgment is what we have been taught and seen modeled all around us, and what has been going on for thousands of years. So we need to be gentle with ourselves if we are having a hard time forgiving. In fact forgiveness is not even something at which we have to make an effort, it occurs naturally when truth is known. That is the value of re-entering the original time period. We have a direct experience, and the resultant expansion in awareness makes all the difference.

Someone once asked me if multi-incarnational work was necessary to clear issues and develop on a soul level, or could it just happen naturally in one's life. My answer was 'both.' Multi-incarnational work just quickens the process.

# More than a Therapy

———————⌘———————

As different lifetimes are revealed, we begin to see recurrent themes and patterns, and to have a sense that our soul line is working on something specific in addition to becoming aware. We have the opportunity to see our unique thread in this magnificent global tapestry. Because multi-incarnational exploration works on so many levels, it can touch places that other therapies cannot, and focused to meet a wide variety of needs.

It can be used to explore more deeply one's **spiritual nature**, one's relationship to the Higher Self. We see stories where there was fear or persecution arising from the activity of communion with our divinity. Old thought forms can be cleared away that define in our minds what spiritually is for us. Does it mean denying the body, the pleasures of sensuality, sexuality? Does it mean perhaps, living a life of poverty or ostracism? Withdrawal to a cave? Is sacrifice a part of our paradigm? Was our God a punishing God? We carry within us the strands of all religions since the beginning of time, no matter what our personal philosophy is now.

Perhaps a person had a lifetime as a healer, sorcerer or scientist where they were involved with exploring and playing with energy; in their current life they may be afraid to touch into that pure energy, afraid they will misuse it or be hurt by it. A great manipulator in business or a seductress is highly developed in the use of energy. They can sense very quickly what is going on in a given situation and use their talents to get what they want. This fluidity and attunement to energy currents can create a great healer or influential speaker. We learn that the energy itself isn't the problem: it's all in how we use it.

People often seek out this work to explore **physical ailments**. They do so with the understanding that we are not looking for cures necessarily, although that can happen; we are interested in the metaphor of that illness/injury. What is it expressing for us? What is it teaching us? What is coming up for us to look at, understand and release? In other words, our body is not our enemy, something separate that we are at the mercy of. The body holds the blueprints of the soul and is an intimate part of who we are and what we are doing here. Emotions not expressed become locked in the cells of our body creating a blocked energy flow. This, then, can manifest as illness. When the block is cleared, health and balance can be restored.

People who come to this work usually understand this. They will say how much they have grown as a result of their affliction, that it is the best thing that ever happened to them. Even diseases like cancer and AIDS, have offered people the opportunity to stop and look at their lives, to heal relationships, to realize what is important and to learn to face death. The main benefit seems to be the awareness of living each moment as fully as possible. A friend called me recently who was in the last stages of AIDS. He told me, 'I've never been happier.'

We are going to die, all of us. Death is the unspeakable of our western culture. When we have come to terms with death; when we can see it as a passage, not an end; when we can understand the eternal nature of the soul that never dies: then life here on earth will be a very different experience. It will not be based on fear but on a joyful expression of who we are and what we can share and create together.

In Multi-Incarnational Therapy we take every lifetime to the death, sometimes even beyond, so the individual has a chance to experience self-continuity. Also, in clearing repetitive patterns around death, such as always dying of heart or chest problems, accidents or head-injuries, we can erase tendencies that have been brought into this life. We don't have to die from illness or accident. We can simply leave when we are ready, creating new paradigms.

Sometimes a theme is expressed in a particular part of the body, as in a fear of stepping forward creating problems in the knees. When this is explored, the problem often disappears. There can even be unexpected bonuses. I once had a client who reported back to me six months later that she had stopped smoking immediately after the sessions. Smoking had never even come up in the sessions but apparently we had dealt with the underlying issue in another way that rippled out to create a shifting of energy. Pretty amazing.

**Life's direction or purpose** is another theme that draws people to this work. There is a growing awareness, a stirring inside, of human possibilities that we have only dreamed of previously. We know there is more that we are capable of doing and becoming. Technology has greatly freed us from having to focus on our daily survival needs. People are understanding they have a gift to give, and wish to give it. Sometimes this involves changing careers, families or geography. Sometimes it simply involves clearing away the blocks to effectively using what is already present in one's life.

A young woman came to me from the Boston area who was involved in teaching young children. This had been her life's dream. She wanted to teach from a perspective of honoring the children and being a guide to their unfoldment. But she ran into opposition from parents and teachers who were more traditional, and found herself feeling very discouraged. She came for sessions questioning her life's purpose. What she discovered were many lifetimes of speaking truth from a place of righteousness and being persecuted for it. She had an air of superiority and condescension about her, so people often reacted negatively to her and her ideas. At the end of her sessions she realized that she didn't want to change professions, she just needed to change her attitudes. She herself needed to honor other people more, including the parents and teachers. She called a few months later to tell me things had improved. She had better communication with the parents and she was much happier. Change ourselves and our reality changes.

Often there are **expectations of success** that draw people to explore their potential. As we hone in on what success means to them personally, we begin to pare away family and cultural definitions of success; money, family, college, beauty, relationships, power, etc.. As the sessions progress, we usually arrive at a definition of success that means being the Self in every moment and expressing that Self in the world. We take the attention away from the outer world, and place it inside. Then the person is free to express outwardly coming from Self's true heart. This brings the peace and happiness they have been seeking and a sense of inner fulfillment.

At the very core of this work is the clearing and understanding of the **emotional body**. This method can be used in a very therapeutic way by going under patterns that are not moving in conventional therapy. Therapies that focus on understanding issues of this life can be helpful in bringing awareness to underlying patterns and themes and how they are played out: but often the patterns continue, even though we can now see and articulate them. At this point we often feel frustrated and powerless. Multi-Incarnational Therapy can help us go deeper and clear our patterns energetically, while simultaneously expanding our view of events and ourselves. It is, in a way, a bridge between the psychological and the spiritual. For those who are ready, it a profound experience.

By seeing our lives, our personal issues, in the context of the history of the species, we feel a part of the evolutionary unfoldment of consciousness expressing itself at the cosmic level.

Very precious.

Issues of fear and distrust, towards self and others, melt away in the embrace of the Divine. A sense of well-being replaces anxiety. Life has meaning and purpose in a way far beyond anything we have been programmed for. We are special just for who we are in this cosmic dance. No measurement, judgment or expectations. We are the greatest force in the universe, the spark of life. We are connected to all it's possibilities — infinite love.

As we melt into this awareness, everything around us changes. Who we are radiates out to touch others in our lives. Relationships heal, work is fun and creativity comes forth to be expressed! The emotional body merged with the light of it's own being can be present in a marvelous new way.

# Consequences of Current actions

The Higher Self will often show us scenarios that enable us to see the consequences of our current actions. If we cannot express our feelings or open our hearts to people in this life, it may show us a lifetime where we had the same behavior and died lonely and miserable. If we only valued wealth and power, it may reveal a story where our wife and family felt emotionally neglected and left us.

Conversely, it can help us remember experiences that were positive and turned out well. The woman, afraid of being free and doing what she wants, may have the experience of being an adventuresome young man going from town to town, doing exactly what he wanted. She can see that nothing bad has to happen and is then able to remember that sense of well-being and freedom in her body. These experiences do carry over into our lives now because they activate cellular memory.

If we are allowed to play out our lives, our themes and issues in a safe environment, we are then in a position to heal fears and go forward, to see that we are more than our problems. We are the Divine Self having a good time here. We must remember this...

# Our Stories

—⟨∞⟩—

## ALICIA
### Clearing her husband Hank
### Victim/Victimizer

Alicia came for sessions immediately following a difficult divorce. Her husband had abused her emotionally and physically, but she still felt herself tied to him in some way. In her sessions she asked for clarity around these issues and the freedom to be herself.

> I see a very large Black man. Dressed only in a loin cloth. Very primitive-looking. It's me. very short, curly, kinky hair — very dark piercing eyes — heavy features, huge hands and feet. Outside. Pretty flat and dry. Africa.
>
> Now I have a spear in my hand and a tribal head-dress on. Still just standing there. Alone. I'm moving toward people who are doing primitive dancing around a fire. I'm much bigger than everyone else. All the men are dancing and the women are sitting around. They don't have clothing on the lower part of their bodies. All very dark.
>
> Now I'm just dragging one of the women by her hair. Just drag her into the tent and rape her. Is a noth-ing act, means really nothing to me. Just the physical brute act. She just lays there, she says nothing. I don't

feel much of anything.

I now sit down and watch the men dancing. The woman comes out and joins her group. She's very sullen. Nobody pays much attention.

I have a mean countenance to myself, unfeeling. I feel empty and very very heavy. I'm afraid inside but I don't know how to change.

I finally get up. Go into this dwelling with the same woman. She's in there. We're living alone in some kind of couple arrangement. I start to feel bad for the way I treat her (It's Hank).

The moment I start to feel badly, I just walk up to her and hit her. It's my fear of giving it up. She doesn't move but she looks directly at me. She doesn't act real afraid, just doesn't move out of the way. She knows and I know she knows — **how deeply I hurt.** Something that's gone on for a long time. But I've started to realize — I've been trying desperately to stop it. No one has ever talked about it. This goes on, accepted, not discussed. It's a very primitive tribe — been very acceptable behavior. Unquestioned.

I was always much bigger. My father did this to me. I don't say anything or do anything about it — my own fear of him. He hits me around the head mostly, no verbal communication, no reason. The anger is just there, not anything I do that's so horrible. I'm 11-12. Gets worse as I get older.

I **hate** him for what he does. But I hate him so long, it's just a way of life. **I pretty well shut down.** It goes into my body, into my muscles. Makes me feel really tight. I pretty much accept it. It's when I'm older now, I realize it's killing me.

In my thinking, I could endure it. I could for a long time.

It stopped as I got older and bigger but by that time, it had a hold of me. I chose to pick on someone weaker than me. I don't direct it to other men, I direct it to her. It made me feel **worthless**. Made me feel **powerful**. The feeling builds up and overwhelms me. I can't contain the fear that I'll be found out. It's a desperate feeling — can't go on like that.

I'm starting to sense something else that's wrong. Feels like a water level is engulfing me. Will win if I don't do something. So heavy — I'll drown in it. It's my own **hatred**, own anger, own **sadness**, **despair**.

I just know I'm going to die if I don't do something about it. **I never felt any love.** I know this woman holds the key. Here I am, this big man and she's the strong one.

I'm sitting there and for the first time in my life, I cry. Throws everybody into shock! Just sit there a long time. I get up and for the first time I move toward my woman, put my hand on her — finally able to touch somebody — to have some kind of feeling for them.

I help her up, she puts her arms around me. She's so relieved. Our son is there, is around 10. Somehow, I didn't take it out on him but he saw me hit his mother so much. I take him in my arms. So relieved I didn't take it out on him. This is the first time I held him as close. Like he'll have a much better chance than I had.

I look so much more alive — looked like this loping animal before. Look more like a man now. All this water inside me is gone. So I feel lighter.

I really saw my wife as having a lot of power, she didn't have much choice, nowhere to go. She cared for me in some way, despite it all. It was this something that kept me alive, like redeemed me. We were a very primitive people with a lot of ritual, not very close to a god or a sense of right and wrong.

Can see myself taking part in the dancing for the first time. The rest notice a change, pay more attention. I don't feel as isolated.

My wife and I have a bond. It's all been worth it. Sex has a warmth that was never there. Like a new world.

I see our little girl, 5-6. She's happy. I'm happy. I'm just happy watching her because I know she won't live in fear of me. This is a relief — I feel a peace, like going from nothing to something. **I'm more than my instincts.** I'm not this cold, hard, impenetrable person.

At death I see myself lying on the ground with a spear in my chest. It was accidental. One of the other men in the tribe — were out hunting. I'm 45. I died quickly — peacefully.

**(From the Higher Self)**

I see the words 'You are light,' coming towards me out of the clouds.

Seeing her husband as the victim and herself the victimizer, was a very healing experience for Alicia: it allowed for a balancing of the power. It also gave her a chance to understand his behavior and to feel compassion for him.

Freedom often occurs in many people following this type of role reversal where they have a chance to experience the other side.

## ILANA
### Fear of Power

Ilana is a vital attractive woman in her early 40's who has been doing healing massage for many years. She is now exploring the possibility of teaching and writing about her work. She feels, however, that something is holding her back. In her sessions, the following lifetimes came forward.

I see a stone wall, running along a country road — nice grass, trees. Most of the land is open but are individual trees — oaks. Looking at it.

Everything went dark — eyes, rapid eye movement — images disappeared — went dark. Still dark.

I'm lying in a coffin, under the earth. Road. I saw a stone wall right near where I'm buried. I'm dead but still attached to that body. I'm a woman — **lot of sadness** coming up. I'm dressed in a black dress, tight bodice, full bottom. Long dark hair, pulled back into a bun. A feeling of loneliness, sorrow. She doesn't quite want to leave that place. Is a lot of sadness.

**She's very powerful.** I am. I'm there, still attached to my body by sheer force of will. I don't want to go on. Such a big feeling in my body. A feeling that if I just lie here in this coffin, I can control the power that's inside. It's a power that I don't want anymore. don't want to live with this power.

It's the power to heal, but also the power to hurt. I feel I've done something despicable, but the scary part of it is — I didn't mean to do it, so it's made me **mistrust the power and fear it**. So, I'm lying here in this coffin, trying not to go anywhere, trying to disappear. But it feels like the power is so strong in this body, that if I just live, it comes out. So I'm glad to be dead.

A suicide. Has to do with my family. They were killed because of me. Was my biological family, husband and two children. Murdered by someone.

I was a very wise woman in a feudal community. Was a healer, also a visionary. People consulted me for advice because I could also see in the probable future. Was a gift I always had, both of them, since I was a child.

Something happened. The feudal lord of the area consulted with me about a battle/confrontation with some neighboring city/state. I told him not to do it, a lot of people would be killed and the battle lost. But he was very angry and went into battle. It happened. He didn't lose the war completely but he lost significantly. In his rage and feeling of frustration, he blamed it on me, said I made it happen. **I was evil.**

So he took me prisoner, but I wasn't afraid. I knew I'd spoken truth, but that enraged him even further. So he had my husband and children taken and murdered and tortured in front of me. Was horrible.

I killed myself, had a poisonous plant or powder. I just wanted to destroy myself. I can't stand it that I'm responsible for the horrible deaths of my family. I could be as righteous as I wanted but it didn't matter. He still had the power over me, that man.

So I just want to die. Staying stuck in this body.

**(From the Higher Self)**

That's a big part of my feeling now that I don't deserve to live. Is a part of me still stuck there, part of my power. I felt that power is a very dangerous thing to have. It's time to re-claim that power. Fear and self-hatred have been running my life for too long — is time to let go. It wasn't my fault that happened.

**IN ANOTHER LIFETIME:**

Could be here in Santa Fe. Very similar but a long time ago. High desert, adobe buildings. Very small dwelling, a hut. Quite a distance from town. I'm an

Indian, very old, lots of wrinkles. In the sun most of my life. Long black, grey hair, dressed in brightly colored but old clothes. Smoking a pipe. Old shaman woman.

Have a little animal living with me. Very at peace, near the end of my life — in late 80's. I'm very in touch with all the spirits of the earth, all the animal spirits, the clouds — with everything. I've just blended into all of it.

Even as a child, I communicated with animals and plants. The animals knew me, related to me different than to others. I could read their minds. People thought I was strange but I fit in with the culture. A lot of these people would come to me for healing, not ordinary things; problems with a sick child or a difficult childbirth — someone regular people couldn't handle. I would do healing ceremonies usually using spirits of animals and plants and working with them to balance what was wrong.

Some parents have brought a very sick child. Are with me in this tiny place. I'm burning some herbs and chanting. I'm in a **very expanded state**. Very connected to the earth and sky.

I'm somehow taking energy from the earth and sky — channelling that energy into the child. It's feverish. The energy is very cooling, very calming. I have my hands on the child. As I continue to chant and channel that cooling energy, I feel I'm one with the earth and sky. Fever starts to leave. The child is healed.

That energy begins to expand inside me. I **feel radiant, connected**, expanded. The Higher Self tells me I **no longer need to be afraid** of this power. I have a gift and it wants to be used. **There is nothing to fear.**

I die peacefully in that life.

In these sessions, Ilana not only had the opportunity to see what she was afraid of, but she also had the experience of standing in her power, peacefully and joyfully.

When I last spoke to her, she has become a successful teacher in her work and is completing her first book.


## JEAN
### Sexuality

Jean's session typifies the ambivalent attitude we have all carried about sexuality. In this life, Jean is very conflicted about her sexuality and presents an androgynous, boyish look to the world. She has lived on an ashram and was in a space of totally suppressing her sexuality and vitality when she came for sessions.

> France, in a bar. I'm a singer and a dancer — strip tease/burlesque, bar — where shows are put on. I'm a dancer and singer. I'm very beautiful — dark hair, large eyes, long eyelashes, fine features. Beautiful lovely figure. Medium height, 5'7". Cute.
>
> I have lots of energy. I enjoy what I'm doing, love every minute of it. It's fun — I love to sing and dance and I love to strip. I feel I have a gorgeous body and I enjoy it! Have a lot of pride in my body. Just an arrogance about it.
>
> So there's a pride in that. Men come to see me — enjoy my body. Is great. Is a highness to that, **a sense of power**. You can tantalize, tease, but done sweetly, humorously, softly. To me, it seems like it's done in good taste.
>
> The audience is all men, mostly upper class — businessmen, doctors, etc. I talk to the people, go out and mingle with the guys in the crowd. some of them

are friends, come a lot. Lot of them are married. But they're not rowdy, distasteful. Gentlemen. In the 1800's.

I own this establishment. There is also prostitution. But it is a really good establishment, kept under good control, good people.

I'm just talking, greeting people that come in, setting them up with the different girls. I don't currently have sex with the customers but I started out that way. I was 20. Just fun. People would sit around and joke, have a good time, have some drinks. We would pair off and go to bedrooms. Very flirtatious. Was a way to make a living. **I like the men.** Basically just a living — getting paid for something I do well. The men don't like their wives, they come for fun. I could do things with them their wives wouldn't do — more free. I enjoyed that — was playful, fun, entertaining. Is a lot of attention in that and a lot of attention given back. **Was a pleasure** in giving in that way and a pleasure in what the men could give. More like an infatuation, not really being in love, but **I loved them.** Nobody in particular.

As I get older, I stop doing the prostitution — get tired of it. Tired of serving the men, the superficiality of it. Lost the zeal but I still enjoyed talking to them. I'm in my middle 50's.

I never married. Was an older man interested in me but I never wanted to get married. Didn't think I could settle down with the kind of life I'd led, wouldn't be fair — **not be a good wife.**

Feel really tired, **didn't feel I had much to give.** Physically lost the desire. Emotionally, not ready, didn't know how. Didn't want to make that commitment.

This man was a decent man. I felt if I married him,

it wouldn't be good. With my reputation and background. Or me, I didn't want that discrimination. Like
I didn't belong in that situation. **I didn't deserve that
kind of respect.**

Youth is gone, talent dies out. **I feel useless, don't
have value.** I can't entertain anyone, so what purpose
is there? All that worthiness was really tied in what I
could do — the body — the ability to make men happy,
what I could do with them.

The people I worked with were like family. Girls
were nice — close knit, took care of each other. so
they took care of me when I got older. The business
was distributed to different partners, so I got to
paint, didn't do much anymore. Retired. Just lived,
stayed fairly healthy. No regrets. Had fun, enjoyed
my life.

Now I feel really sad. **Have doubt.** Wondered if it
would have been better if I'd married, had a family. I
question, what kind of love did I really give? I died
that way. Asking God for forgiveness for any wrong
doings I had done. Really wasted my life.

These feelings came as I got older and could observe more. Though everybody took care of everybody,
it still seemed a selfish lifestyle. I always wondered if
something else had more meaning to it.

**(From the Higher Self)**
Don't deny the love that was in your heart at that time,
what you gave.

In this experience, Jean was able to release her self-judgment
and feeling of unworthiness. She re-claimed her joy in giving, and
pleasure in her female body.

## SUSAN
### Soul's Purpose

In a session to explore life's purpose, the grandfather is the guide.

**Grandfather** comes in as a being full of radiant flames — a human outline, but barely. I'm seeing him as **flaming light energy**, kind of like a square outline, but fiery. I don't see his face, seems to be an energetic form. Raw power, raw energy. Moving energy, burning energy. Very **alive and powerful** — like the burning bush.

I feel intrigued to see where we're going to go and what he's got to show me. He has a quality of experience I want.

Seems to be a god realm. Where the Greek gods hang out — Zeus and those guys. Lightening coming out of their hands. A male figure in a cloak — fiery. A Zeus-like Greek pantheon up in the clouds — temples, gods lying around in togas, playing around with the Earth. The Earth is a plaything and they are playing with forms.

I've been here a lot, creating different creatures. This is **power**, we're dealing with here. When I look into this Zeus character, I look out through him into the universe, into another realm. Very electrical, high vibration — ecstatic energy. Like he's the gateway.

We're going out into this space. My grandfather's taking my hand and we're going through this place. We're going out on this planet of fire. It's very ecstatic, electrical, and orgasmic. Like flames of light — bliss — light. He's standing on it and he is grounded on it. He is that energy and he invites me to stand there with him and let that energy flow up through my feet, into my body. **I am ready to be grounded in this divine flame,** divine intelligence of all that is. Very powerful. The **power of God** and I'm just standing in it — and it's taking me over — and I'm becoming it.

It's a current of pleasure, fast electrical, sweet electrical — powerful and sweet and full and rich. Like plugging into voltage without it hurting. The voltage is glowing through me, pure energy. My body is streaming, creates a tingling. It is aligning with that pure vibration, full and rich, nothing else needed.

My grandfather is saying, 'MORE and MORE — turn up the voltage now.' I am able to abide in it. My body just slips into it very comfortably. Home. It's what I've always known. With my feet, I tap into this burning light. Like I am this burning bush and I am consumed by it. It is expanding. I have absolutely no fear. My body just welcomes it in.

He keeps saying, 'MORE!' I am aligning to it and becoming it. I feel myself going deep into this planet. I feel it a lot in my lower torso, really burning and tingling. My grandfather is nodding his head. It's almost, as he stands there with me, it anchors me more. He's confident in it. He's serving as a grounding wire as I match him.

As I stand in this, I experience incredible joy, incredible opening of the heart — like a fountain opening up and shooting. This is all there is, there is no resistance, full surrender. Just the fullness of the light body. It's under all of the rest — my God Self.

It's already there in my daily life. I'm already doing it. All I need to do is just allow and trust, not worry about how I'm received. This is taking over. It is now in my beingness, and **I'm not stopping it up anymore, holding it back or apologizing for it.**

It is expressed through me as a passion, joy, excitement, aliveness, clarity, energy, inspiration. It's all opened up. My job is just to allow it.

He just became a comet and shot off. We're two comets shooting out into the galaxy. Pure light, pure fiery light.

Now I am going to a humongous sun. And this sun has an intelligence, consciousness — more than the other place — the home of cosmic intelligence. It's huge! — brilliant beyond brilliant! The comet goes right inside, going back to source. The frequency of the comet is the same as this huge sun.

A heartbeat. The divine heart

My grandfather's saying, 'Now that you are here, you don't need me.' He is blended into this energy. I feel my heart opening, becoming very very warm, and there's a lot of expansion going on in the chest. That fire is taking over the heart and spreading out the boundaries of the heart. My sense of a connection to a vast intelligence. It's deepening into something deeper — to a more profound connection, an attunement... The place where I wake up in the middle of the night. Slipping back in the essential being. I'm sitting/standing right in the middle of it. Like the Higher Self expanded 100 million times! Deep, warm, pulsating radiance in the heart. It keeps pulling me in deeper and deeper, making it more real to me — taking my attention. It is wordless. It is all. It is wonderful to be standing in this place that I usually just touch. I'm really immersed in it. It's pulling me deeper.

Grandfather says, 'Go deeper! There's nothing in the way. It's all open to me now.' My heart's on fire. I'm in a place where I'm ready to live it. **That's what I've come to do.** Message is: keep deepening. All is there — at the focal point in the heart. There's a flame of light rising up into my heart, That flame is like an anchor, like an umbilical cord back to the source.

The exploration begins. The real exploration begins of this. The Self that I am, that I came in with. The teacher, the knower — the energetic beingness underlying the personality self.

My grandfather is saying, 'This is what your father had in him, but he couldn't do it. It's the power of the anger; he got lost in it.' But I'm doing it. He's happy with me, has a twinkle in his eye. But, also what I'm doing that he couldn't do, **is bring it through the heart**. Like I'm a culmination of the lineage. They gave me the gifts of financial security so I can explore these depths.

I feel a sense of this great sun being. Allness. Feel it in my heart and it's becoming my whole body. Every cell is becoming that, absorbing, aligning, remembering this. Everything is there, the knowing, abundance, and love. Every cell is complete in itself. nothing has to be added to this.

Over and over I get the message: 'there's nothing in the way.' I feel like a Buddha, full of light.

I am writing this book as an outcome of this session...

*Part Three*

---

# The Higher Self in Life: Coming Home

# Living It

———— ∽ ————

There is a phrase circulating these days, 'Walk your talk.' We seem to be increasingly impatient with ourselves and others who say one thing and do another. We are more demanding of our teachers and leaders. We want them to reflect and live their teachings, not just talk about them. As children, many of us were told by our elders, 'Do as I say, not as I do.' This inconsistency in behavior has been confusing and frustrating for those doing it as well. Hasn't each of us been in a situation where we believed one way and acted another?

Perhaps our impatience is reflecting a place of readiness as a species to shift consciousness, to manifest truly what we know we are, individually and collectively. Considering the expansion of our brain capacity and the growing knowledge of human behavior, we are now in a position heretofore unknown on this planet: a place of INTEGRATION. All of what we have experienced and learned is in the ethers and in every cell of our bodies. We are ready to live on all levels — spiritually, emotionally and physically — what we have intuitively known is possible.

So the question is, how can we put our knowledge into practice? How can we move from mental understanding to actual realization? Much of what has been presented in this book has the intention of taking theoretical material and creating bridges, making the Inner Self tangible and alive for us in our everyday lives. It is in the present moment that we live, not some phantasied future. This is what counts: right here, right now. There **are** some guidelines...

# The Power of Intention

Intention is everything. There is really nothing we have to do but desire the connection to Self more than anything. And it will take the strength of that intention to cut through the many habits and distractions that have been undermining Self since birth. It is a big job, but not impossible. When the call to wake-up begins deep in our hearts, the power of the universe is called into play. There comes a momentum fueled by pure love, and we have lots of help.

So, how do we create intention? What is it that happens when a person says, 'Enough, I've had it with the way my life is going. I want off this merry-go-round.' Some people call it grace. One cannot predict when the passion to know the Self will arise.

I hear many people expressing the desire for divine communion, yet they continue to place their attention elsewhere. I once worked with a physician who deeply longed for attunement with his spiritual nature. He was a thoughtful, gentle man who cared deeply about people. In past-life sessions, he slipped easily into oneness with his Higher Self and there he experienced great joy and peace. We repeatedly explored his fears around groups and expressing truth. Walls crumbled from around his heart and he was able to open to the great love he felt for his family. However, he felt compelled to close off connection to Self when he returned home. Living in a very conservative community, he was terrified of the ostracism that might follow if he truly lived from his heart. As time went on, he resisted inner communion and self-nourishment, not taking the time to check in with himself or to create a lifestyle that would allow him fuller expression. Not only did he have a passion for art that he longed to express, he also had innovative ideas for compassionate ways to be with his patients. The last I heard, some of these latter ideas were being implemented and he was making quite a difference in his community. But on a personal level he was still having the experience of running all the time, unwilling to take the time to meditate or just 'be.' He continued to give attention to his fears. I trust this man will slow down and tune into himself when the time is right. The seeds of truth have been activated. Life has its own timetable and I have come to honor that.

I suggest two ways to help you become aware of your intention:

1. Stop periodically through the day, paying close attention to your thoughts, behaviors and activities. Become aware of yourself as an impartial observer. Where are you putting your energy?

2. Be honest with yourself if you still have interest in playing out certain patterns. It's OK. The time may not be ready for letting go. Timing is everything.

The gurus talk about 'ripening,' a readiness for surrender/awakening. Other teachers describe the need for a prepared consciousness. Who can know? The desire to awaken can start in childhood or come in a flash on a crowded city street. That is grace.

Wherever you are in your life, if the desire for freedom is stirring deep inside, you are ready. The way for you will be revealed. I suggest you 'fan the flame' of this desire and it will consume all other desires.

# Wake-up Call: Winds of Change

Something is stirring throughout the planet, a gentle current encouraging us to awaken. In my work I have traveled to many countries and seen people from all over the world: the politician from Washington, the computer analyst from Japan and the woman living on a farm in Iowa. People come from many occupations: physicians, lawyers, CEO's, housewives, teenagers, children, airline pilots, scientists, psychologists, engineers, teachers, fashion models, artists, and musicians. It is not just people 'on the fringe' who are exploring their multi-dimensional nature, but average everyday people who are the inner pulse of our society.

Some people describe their process as an 'alarm clock going off' inside their heads. 'It's time.' One man reported that his wife had been trying to get him to read books on personal growth and spirituality for years. He just wasn't interested, thinking it was all that 'New Age stuff.' Then, one morning, he woke up and started reading the books she had lying around the house. He discovered an insatiable hunger to go inside and know more about himself and the deeper meaning of why he was here. He looked at me and laughed, 'A year ago, I wouldn't have been caught dead doing work like this, but here I am, and I'm happy to be here. It's been the most important year of my life.'

An airline pilot talked about 'being in the closet' for 20 years, in relation to his spirituality. He spoke of it to no one, and it was his secret from family and friends who were very traditional. When he came to do multi-incarnational sessions, he was surprised at how normal we facilitators were. When I asked him what he had expected, he said 'I don't know, flowing robes or something.' A businessman from New York commented that he saw exploring the Inner Self as the new challenge, the leading edge. He had done the outer exploration, and now it was time to do the **inner** exploration.

Interest in this kind of inner work can be found in unlikely places. I was visiting my daughter in Detroit, Michigan one Thanksgiving, and we went to have dinner with her boyfriend's family. They lived in Dearborn, a small town on the edge of Detroit which has a reputation for being highly resistant to anyone and anything different. My daughter implored me as we approached the house, 'Please, Mom, don't tell them what you do...' As we were sitting around the dinner table, which included the strict Italian grandmother, the mother and father, and grown children, the inevitable question arose, 'And Mrs. Harris, what is it you do... ?' I took a deep breath, checked inside and heard a 'yes,' and proceeded to describe my work. My daughter glared at me.

When I was done, there was a silence, then the grandmother shrieked out in delight — 'I've always wanted to do that work. I've read all of Shirley McLaine's books, and I find past-life experiences so fascinating!' The family all looked at her in shock. Then something shifted in them and they, too, began to ask animated questions about past-lives and other spiritual issues. Needless to say, my daughter heaved a great sigh of relief.

Speaking of Shirley McLaine, I have great admiration for her inquiry into the spiritual realm. Having been present at many of the experiences she describes in her books I find her reporting to be accurate. She is an intelligent, skeptical investigator of truth. In addition, she has opened people up to valuing their own spiritual experiences. Over and over, people have come to me saying, 'if Shirley can talk about it, I can talk about it.'

There is a sense of things speeding up, changing. People can feel this in their lives. Whatever is not aligned with truth is becoming uncomfortable and can't be suppressed as easily as before. This involves relationships, work situations, and personal freedom. Volcanoes are erupting, the 'winds of change' are blowing. If we don't resist these currents, we can move into new realms of experience that create more joy and aliveness than we have ever known. It is said 'where there is no resistance, there is no harm.' We can learn to 'go with the flow.'

# Surrender

───────────────◦○◦───────────────

Surrender has been talked about as a necessary component of most religious and spiritual disciplines. It means many things to many people. Too often, it has meant giving up our personal will to an outside authority who is supposed to know our truth better than ourselves. As a result, many people tremble at the idea of surrender. We have not had good experiences around this issue. To many of us, it means 'giving up.'

I see surrender as coming home to the Self — or recognizing the authority of the Inner Self in all situations. To let go into the divine moment, allowing life to be guided by this ultimate wisdom and intelligence. To die to the limited ideas of self and to give birth to the infinite possibilities of who we really are. Surrender is realizing what has always been true and involves simply a shift in perception.

## WHO IS THE DOER?
In Western society, we are particularly fond of the ego, or individualized self. Individuality is our touchstone. We feel patriotic about free enterprise and proud of our personal initiative. We strongly identify with our personalized self that we feel is unlimited, knowing it to be a great part of our communal strength. In America, we do not feel bound by tradition and politics like other countries. Our ancestors came here for personal freedom and it has paid off for us. Well, almost... Somewhere, along the way, we seem to have lost touch with the spiritual spark that so ignited the founders of this great country. In

our desire to create, develop and conquer, we have lost our inner connection and become out of balance as a nation.

Being so strongly identified with our ego self we are reluctant, even frightened to let go of it. If we surrender to the Inner Self, we wonder, will we become like monks in a cave, withdrawn and passive in the world? Will we only want to sit around and contemplate our navel? We see life in extremes; active or passive. We can't imagine 'not doing.' It is the American way. The trouble is, we are 'doing' ourselves into heart disease, cancer, obesity and alcoholism; all diseases associated with being unable to slow down and be at peace with ourselves. When I was in Europe a few years ago, someone asked me why we were having so much crime and social problems in the United States. Out of my mouth, spontaneously came, 'We have lost touch with our soul.'

We think we are the 'doer': that it is our intelligence, talent and energy that make things happen. But really, 'Who is the doer?' We may need to go through a humbling process that acknowledges the mysterious force that activates all creativity and productivity, the intelligence that inspires us to scientific breakthroughs and innovative technology. A being that is ever-present, guiding every activity and opportunity.

The creative person is aware of this intuitive process. Inventors talk about breakthroughs coming in their dreams or by accident. Entrepreneurs manage 'by the seat of their pants' or through their 'gut reaction.' Call it what you will, it is divine inspiration.

Recently, a close friend of mine related a story wherein she totally surrendered to the pulsation of life. It happened during a week-long workshop in which she was working on her control themes. As she explored fears of letting go, something happened, and she went into an altered state. In that state, she trusted in the rightness and perfection of each moment; intellectual measurement was gone. There was no moment better than the next, so each event was perfect. Fear of death was suspended and a feeling of safety permeated every moment. There was nothing for her to 'do' but just be present in that: to be talked, moved and created by this force, moment to moment. In fact, there was no separation between 'her' and 'it.'

What she experienced that week was a profound sense of peace and lightness she had never before felt, where everything was in harmony. Throughout this magical time, she realized she didn't have the bigger picture, that something far greater, far more loving and intelligent was in charge guiding the show. Most importantly, she knew she wasn't the doer, she wasn't in control. Such a feeling of peace...

After that week, much of her sense of expansion faded although she did retain the awareness of the perfection of each moment, no one moment better than another.

So, what happened? Why is it she couldn't retain this experience of such peace and joy? This is a problem many of us run into after knowing great expansiveness.

## THROWING AWAY THE JEWEL

Some of the answer lies in becoming aware of our cultural selectivity. In Western cultures, we simply don't relate to spiritual experiences. We end up throwing them away, invalidating them. We don't have a paradigm that knows the power of surrender: we don't have support from those around us who value the inner life. It is like the parable of the miner who doesn't recognize the worth of the diamond he has just unearthed, so he throws it on the dung heap. That is what we do. When we have an experience of inner radiance we don't understand the incredible gift we have just received. We say to ourselves. 'Ho hum, just another experience. Now, back to our life.' We must learn to cherish these precious gifts and nourish their continual expansion. For this reason, Eastern mystics emphasize the value of a teacher. The teacher can validate your experience, concretize and help you to deepen it.

I find that peak experiences periodically come into our lives to remind us of what is possible. Then, we have to do the inner work in order to remove what's in the way of allowing that expanded awareness as a continuous current in our daily lives. We haven't really lost anything though it feels that way. We have simply turned our attention back to what feels normal to us. Unfortunately, what feels normal is often our pain and struggle.

There was a time when I did not like the idea of surrender. The definition of surrender as 'falling into a black void' was not too appealing to me. A couple of years ago, someone said to me in passing: 'When you surrender, you fall into the arms of God, of love.' That felt a lot better. I could do that.

## ACKNOWLEDGING

In order to re-claim our birthright as spiritual beings, we're going to have to stop and recognize for ourselves the daily miracles in our lives, to lift the scrim of dullness off our eyes and see the presence that is shining back at us. The more we can acknowledge that presence, the fuller our lives will be.

In the Jewish religion, every bite of food is acknowledged to be of God; every activity and event is a blessing, be it positive or negative. Ancient pantatheistic belief sees the God force in nature; every rock, animal and cloud.

God is everywhere. God is us. There is nowhere that God isn't.

This awareness must be seen and recognized in our daily lives in order to be real for us. Going to church once or twice a week, or meditating for an hour a day, isn't enough. One needs to see, really see fresh in the moment, the miracle of life, of this planet, of each other. Every single moment.

## I WORSHIP AT THE FEET OF...

To facilitate the process of surrender, it is helpful to closely examine what we are attached to or 'what do we worship?'

- beauty, love, relationships
- judgment, analysis
- desires, needs, entertainment, stimulation
- achievement, productivity, power

- superiority, inferiority
- ego, separation
- worry, fear
- avoidance, denial, distraction
- safety, control, protection
- doubt, distrust
- being good, acceptance, approval
- being bad, rebellion, anger

We may honestly feel we want a spiritual connection, but most often our attention is focused elsewhere. Going within involves a clarity and honesty with ourselves. What do we really want? Often people are shocked when they step back and soberly look at where they are placing their attention. Just study your thoughts for a few days and you will see for yourself. Truth is not far away.

We are so good at excuses! 'I don't have time to meditate — too busy.' Just even stopping to relax and go within for a few minutes seems superfluous, even scary. 'Not necessary. I have other more important things to do.' What? What is more important than stopping to commune with the love inside that is there to caress us, soothe our wounds, and support us on all levels? What can be more reassuring than noticing the underlying current of our existence that is permanent, everlasting? Taking the time to be in nature drinking in its sounds, smells, textures, and rhythms; palpating the harmony and connectedness that nature embodies. 'I'll do it later,' we say to ourselves.

We are caught up in a mass cultural hypnotism that seems embarrassed about its inner life. We do not do these things and we don't see others doing them (or talking about them), except in New Age circles or in religious communities. Going within somehow seems different and foreign to us.

If we are serious with ourselves, we can explore where we put our time and energy. What do we worship at the feet of...? Our job, relationships, food, guilt, avoidance? By looking at where our repetitive thinking is focused, we bring the light of awareness into what has been unconscious, automatic. This act in itself, allows for a shifting. We become free to make new choices based on our truest heart, to ask ourselves, 'Is this activity what I really want?' It is not hard, but it does take self-awareness and commitment to change.

> Nowadays, I catch myself more and more
> frequently, which is a start. The 'roof-brain
> chatter' is slowly being replaced with a
> stillness that keeps me in the present. Once
> the momentum is broken, the habit will soon wither.
> We have only to remember...Remembering helps
> us to overcome our addiction to 'getting ahead.'
> For when we experience a true present, that is where
> everything happens.
>
> — *Ralph H. Blum*
> Book of Runes[4]

# Releasing Old Structures & Beliefs

---

We have to do our work. The only thing that stands in the way of our being in the divine stream every moment, is our involvement in the planetary hypnotism and the beliefs we have internalized that have become our personal reality. Once these empty structures are seen for the illusion they really are, we have to be willing to **act** on our discoveries. As our ideas about truth change, so will our lives.

We are, indeed, the masters...

# Being Selfish

Our deepest fear is not that we are inadequate. Our deepest fear is that we are powerful beyond measure. It is our light, not our darkness, that most frightens us.

We ask ourselves. Who am I to be brilliant. Gorgeous. Talented. Fabulous. Actually, who are you not to be? You are a child of God. Your playing small does not serve the world.

There is nothing enlightened about shrinking so that other people won't feel insecure around you. We were born to make manifest the glory of God that is within us. It is not just in some of us. It is in everyone.

And as we let our own light shine, we unconsciously give other people permission to do the same. As we are liberated from our own fear. Our presence automatically liberates others.

— *Nelson Mandella*
*1994 Inaugural Speech*
*from* A Return to Love *by Marrianne Williamson* [5]

The fear of being 'selfish' has been a curse on us humans for as long as we can remember. It is a given societal rule: to be selfish is to be bad, possibly the worst thing we can do. We hear this condemnation from our parents at the earliest age, and it is later repeated by teachers and ministers. This fear follows us into personal relationships, and occupational pursuits. As parents we are terrified, 'God forbid I should be selfish and think of my own needs.' Thinking this way literally cripples our psyches in areas far beyond our conscious awareness.

The fear of being 'selfish' is based on a lie, a big fat lie, that we have swallowed and passed on from generation to generation: it says it is not all right to think of ourselves, to let Self be our primary reference point. Accepting this lie is perhaps the worst violation we have done to ourselves as a species. Degradation of Self is of such magnitude that our lives have been affected in every way imaginable. At its core is denial of the Self: to be selfish is to think of the Self; if we are not selfish, we have to deny the Self.

Here we observe the ultimate form of control. If we accept this lie as truth, then we are open to being controlled by others. When we turn away from our own knowing, we have to rely on what others tell us is true. If we believe ourselves to be unworthy, then we have to try to atone, doing things for others. Someone once said, 'Trying to be good is based on the belief that we are bad.' So, we may perform acts of kindness, but without the involvement of the heart the act often feels empty, coming from a place of duty.

Fear of being selfish is perhaps at the root of our personal and social problems, the cancer that eats away at us. If we believe thinking of the Self is bad or expressing the Self in the world is dangerous, then we become the ship without an anchor. We are at sea in the world of sensations, demands, and stimulations with no way to react authentically. We are at the whim of those who can create some semblance of order or purpose. At the heart of control is the essence of separation. Once we become alienated from our own center, our own heart, then we can do anything to others and they can do anything to us. Thus we become an alienated society, separate from ourselves and separate from each other.

From an historical perspective, there is good reason to be suspicious of the individual self. From the outside, it appears to be the self that has created so much misery and chaos on this planet. We have been cruel, callous, violent, and destructive. Acts of greed and jealousy have littered our history with physical and emotional excesses. Our desires have seemed insatiable, our behaviors indulgent. To trust ourselves and each other would be idiotic, we think, since we are so filled with complexities and demons. It seems a contradiction to honor and love the self.

Therein lies the paradox. We are talking here about honoring the Essential Self, not the emotional self with whom we are so identified. This requires going deeper beyond our habits and desires to the underlying current of consciousness, purity and light. There we find the inner radiance that has been hidden by our attending survival behaviors.

Denial of the Self has arisen from ignorance and misunderstanding of our true identity: we thought we were our emotional bodies, our personality selves. This confusion about Self has been exploited by people throughout history who wanted to manipulate and control us.

Alice Miller has written several books on education. She quotes textbooks describing methods intended to suppress the Self in the child at all costs. The motivation is not even hidden, its purpose being to break the will of the child and replace it with acquiescence to authority. I could readily understand when she gave examples from German books on education, but when she referred to American textbooks, it was chilling to me, a little too close to home. I have come to see that not any one country has ownership over suppressive behavior, even though it may be acted out dramatically. The tyrant is in all of us.

However, we are its victim in the most profound sense. The beliefs we have about others come back to us like a rubber band. If we see the inner will/inner self as savage, dangerous, undisciplined and evil, that is how we will view ourselves. This assumption is insidious: it grows and affects every other part of our lives — our personalities, behaviors, self-image, life choices, parenting and our basic emotional states.

There is a term in Psychology called 'healthy selfish' relating to activities that arise from the Inner Self, not the emotional body. It recognizes the existence of a unique authentic Self underneath our conflicts that deserves expression. When this Essential Self is honored and allowed to be present, it hurts no one. It is only filled with impartial truth. It sees the bigger picture so activities that arise from it always create balance, even if it doesn't feel like that at the time. How many instances in our lives have we looked back on situations that were traumatic and commented on how good it was for us that it happened? Our lives were then taken in a different direction. It's almost as if we have to get shaken up once in awhile. Pain only happens when we resist or hold on.

I find that often when a person attacks another for being selfish, it is usually the other way around. The person attacking is usually wanting you to do something **their** way; they are trying to control you. This form of manipulation is frequently used in relationships with parents and children and also between marriage partners. Guilt and resentment are the outcomes.

When we truly act from our own inner rhythms and take the time to be in communion with Self, the results are magnificent. People living this way are a joy to be with. They are truthful, loving, impartial and fun. Life is lived spontaneously but not impulsively: wisdom permeates every action. There is friendliness and honoring of others. It is the opposite of selfishness as we know it. It is the most beautiful thing we can do: bringing the Self here, into life, and knowing this is really the greatest gift we can give to each other.

# Rules of Life

I was sitting on the beach at a small island in the Bahamas, looking out over the crystalline blue-green water and white sandy beach that went on for miles. Warm breezes flowed over my body. I was there with a group of colleagues for a workshop and birthday celebration, so the event was both business and pleasure. Sitting there alone, I examined the discomfort I was feeling inside. Foremost was the question, 'I am in paradise, a place most people only dream of. What's wrong with me? Why can't I be happy and have a good time like the rest of the guests? Why can't I center myself?' I was feeling much self-doubt and confusion.

Gradually I became aware of thinking there were rules to this game called life that I had somehow never learned. As a child I found other people's behavior and value systems very confusing. 'They' seemed to know how to act with each other and in the world, as if they had the rule book and I didn't. Therefore, I felt lost, alone, awkward and confused through much of my childhood. If only I could find the right way to do things, I thought. So, I studied people like laboratory animals, becoming an observer of human nature. What were those secrets?

As I sat on the beach pondering these thoughts, a wisdom rose from deep inside, 'There are no rules, just be who you are.' That realization knocked me over, and I sobbed for hours.

What had I accepted that had totally governed my life and self esteem? Further, I thought, what have we all accepted in order to make sense of our reality and to 'fit in?' I have since discovered that many people have experienced similar feelings. No one seems to have fit in. Interesting...

The message is given to us early in life: there are rules here on planet Earth to which we had better conform or there are dire consequences. As children, we are deeply influenced by the consensus reality passed from generation to generation. This reality contains rules of behavior and value/belief systems: how we're supposed to live, love and think — even what we're supposed to look like.

Rules, rules, rules. There is even a rule for which fork to use, rules for what to say and how to say it. 'Don't talk back,' 'that's not nice.' Rules invade the inner world: 'it is not loving to think like that'; 'you should love your brother,' (who is beating up on you). We're told, 'you're too quiet,' or 'you can't even be still.' All of this is around some standard that we have to measure up against or fit into. 'They say,' or 'they won't like you.' Who are 'they?'

Righteousness has been regarded as a moral virtue growing from our need to make sense of our experience. We have structured our societies around behavior we considered 'right,' and punished those doing things 'wrong.' In more primitive times, we probably needed a strict code of behavior to maintain some semblance of order since our inner consciousness was not well developed. However, these codes have become anachronisms and now function in such a way as to deny life rather than support it.

Scientists tell us there is an energy matrix that we enter at birth which carries all the thinking, feeling, and value systems that will impinge on us during that lifetime. It's like opening a door to a particular reality and stepping in. Once inside, it feels like the only truth.

Years ago, I remember having a conversation with a rabbi. We were both serving on a Human Relations Committee. Knowing that I was interested in spiritual exploration, he told me of an experience he had when he was a younger man. He was deep in meditation one morning, when he became filled with pure light, radiance and love. Ecstasy filled him and this feeling continued for several hours. It was what the mystics call a 'transcendent experience.' The rabbi looked at me with light shining in his eyes as he remembered the exquisiteness of that moment. I was also deeply moved.

After a silence, I asked him if he shared this experience with his congregation. He quickly looked at me, sobered up, tightened his body and replied, 'Of course not, my job as a rabbi is to teach the Law of God.'

I was amazed. I thought, this is why many people are leaving the temples and churches. We have almost totally moved away from the spiritual realm into rules and laws that have very little meaning for contemporary life. We desperately want to be shown the way back to the light, not the rules.

I felt badly for this man who now spoke with eyes glazed over in sadness. He knew what he had thrown away.

While rules may be necessary to govern a society, they are not as beneficial on a personal level. Excessive rules diminish the spirit and create an inner paralysis. Vitality and creativity are not allowed to come forward. Love is limited where there is righteousness: joy is lost. It is a sorry state.

Jerry, a former boyfriend, taught me much about rules and helped me to burn through this issue. He had a rule or a 'right way' to do everything. Studying this issue as a child, he decided to find the right way to do everything. His parents had neglected him emotionally, totally consumed with their own problems. As a result, Jerry became the parent and raised himself. Finding the right way to do things was a survival issue. He had a right way to organize a kitchen, drive a car, make a bed or eat; a right way to start a fire, build a house, plant a garden; a right way to dress and decorate a house. He became angry and critical when things weren't done right, his fear expressed as a superior attitude towards anyone who didn't measure up to his expectations.

Of course, this was a perfect match for someone like me who was sure she had somehow never learned the rules of life. I was caught up in this spin for awhile and then rebelled. Needless to say, the relationship ended. But what a teaching! What a great gift he gave me! Feelings or intuition didn't enter the picture nor creatively living in the moment: all the things I hold dear. I had the opportunity to see the great pain and insecurity underlying Jerry's arrogance. He felt emptiness that he tried to fill with activities. It was very hard for him to be still. Our break-up was painful for me as it is when we are clearing deep life issues. I thank him now.

Since the realization in the Bahamas, my life has dramatically changed. My attention is more on valuing and expressing my inner life, and trusting that what I need to know about the outside world will come to me as needed. It does not have to be 'either/or.' I do not have to deny myself to live in the world. Both are possible, both are necessary in order to live a rich experience here.

The rules of life are open to question, to change. They can be played with and discarded when they don't enhance love and life. Inner and outer are not really different: all one being, all one energy. Rules and structures can enhance life when they are allowed to be fluid, when they come from the heart.

I now know there is no single way that life has to be lived: it is 'your' way. Nobody has the answers or rules for anybody else. As healers and friends, we can help people to facilitate their understanding and unfoldment, but truth always has to come from within each person. This means we are going to have to give up our sense of righteousness. This is particularly difficult for people like myself who are in the healing and teaching professions, since we think we know from an 'enlightened place' what other people need. We may be knowledgeable about human behavior and what creates harmony, but that's not always the point. Everyone has an inner rhythm, a unique Higher Self guiding them perfectly through life. We can share what we are moved to share, and then let go. It is not our business what happens. This approach doesn't mean we don't care, it simply means we know how to trust in something far beyond the mind and it's rules.

I remember the message of the Higher Self 'just be who you are.' It is imprinted in my heart.

# Unworthiness

'I can't do it myself. I'm not good enough!'

An incident happened to me about 20 years ago that has stayed with me. It embodied my self-judgment and the feeling of worthlessness that was underneath.

Following my divorce, I dated a man who I was certain was my true love. He was also a psychotherapist and seemed to have everything I was searching for in a man. He was tender, loving, sensitive, attractive and extremely intelligent. So to my surprise, I found myself liking him less and less, feeling unhappy about many of the things he did. Since we usually shared our feelings, I decided to tell him how I felt. After I read off my list of things I was unhappy about, he looked at me with sadness in his eyes. He said, 'Susan, you seem to want a lot of things from me that I can't give. What is that about for you?.'

I was furious with him for putting the problem back on me rather than addressing his own 'grievous sins.' I was sure he was the problem, not me.

Alone, later, I tried to explore my anger and pain. After venting my anger with pillows about how he wasn't what I needed him to be 'for me,' I touched into deeper pain. This pain caused me to lie on my couch kicking and screaming like a two year old: 'I don't want to do it myself; I don't want to meet my own needs; I can't! I can't! I'm not good enough; I can't do it myself. I don't know how to be happy myself!'

As these words came out of my mouth, I heard them and knew they were true. I had felt that way all my life; it was the cry of the two year old child who had judged herself insufficient, unworthy, not good enough. And if that was the case, then somebody else was going to have to do it for me. As I grew into a woman, that somebody became focused on the current man in my life. Woe be to him...!

Another incident occurred during the same time period, more

subtle, but just as meaningful. I was sitting in my living room staring at the furnishings with no particular emotion. A friend came into the room, walked over to a vase of flowers sitting next to me and exclaimed with delight, 'Look at those beautiful flowers!' All of a sudden, these flowers took on a life, importance, value. They weren't important if it was 'just me.' Again, I knew inside what I was witnessing — my own unworthiness.

How many times do we value somebody else's experience more than our own, even when it's the same event/house/clothing/car, etc.. We feel that what we have or do isn't as good as someone else, or the opposite: what we have is better than someone else's. It's all the same thing. Just the other side of the coin of judgment.

In my work with people over the years, I have found the same fears living in their hearts. I have come to realize that it is the belief in our unworthiness that prevents us from knowing and living from our own radiant center. We simply don't feel we are good enough, so our attention goes outside ourselves to lovers, authorities and 'things.'

When this give-away is seen for what it is, our own personal sell-out, we can gain back the 'kingdom of God.' It has never gone anywhere: it has always been inside us. We were the ones who turned away from our essential goodness and beauty. How lovely to re-claim this, to know that we are more than enough; we are 'All That Is.'

There is a helpful affirmation to work with every day upon rising to help dissolve the energy of judgment:

'I am grateful for everything that comes my way and have no complaints at all.'

As you say this, feel the energy softening in your heart and the sense of openness that happens. Your energy will shift to peace, love and appreciation, away from the tightness and hardness of judgment.

There are no mistakes, nothing is wrong, including ourselves. Life can be lived fully in each perfect moment. Try it...

# Religion or 'The Great Train Robbery'

Organized religion has been the greatest perpetuator of suppressing the Self since the beginning of time. Sometimes the motivation was innocent, but most often it was fueled by greed and power.

At their inception, all the world's great religions carried the seeds of truth, acknowledging the Divine Self in some way. Judaism explained the idea of one God whose scope was too vast to be limited by a name, its substance being light. Christianity arose from the sage Jesus, who taught the necessity of love and forgiveness. He also understood our oneness with divine nature, 'you can do what I can do, and more.' Buddha practiced the awareness of One Self, and the realization that we simply need to be still and go within to know the power of the divine.

Truth has always been with us, but we have distorted and manipulated it for our own benefit.

> The concept of all-sufficiency was a building block of essentially all philosophical and religious systems (in their original form) until the second century A.D. when war against self-knowledge and self-reliance began.

> The Ancients taught that to understand one's self was to understand God, and through the process of meditation, one could release divine energy from within and transmute discord into harmony, ignorance into wisdom, fear into love, and lack into abundance...

> In A.D. 180, Irenaeus, Bishop of Lyons, attacked independent thinking and all teachings related to the Oneness of God and man. Believing that a spiritual consciousness and a personal union with God would undermine the authority of the priests, he directed his wrath upon Gnosticism...The shift in mind-direction

from within to without had begun, and the innate power of the individual was gradually given to an outer structure and a lower authority...The Institution assumed complete control over individual minds and humanity entered the thousand year period referred to as the Dark Ages.

—*John Randolph Price*
The Abundance Book[6]

One does not have to go far back into the world's history to see the most atrocious acts committed 'in the name of God.' The fear and hatred that have arisen when one group of people thought they had the only truth. Righteousness says, 'I am right, and you are wrong,' often adding, 'If you don't convert or agree with me, I will kill you.'

Christianity is to me, the most amazing example of all. When it began, an incredible wave of love swept the planet. Its teacher, Jesus, awoke the heart to gentleness and compassion. His teachings were simple and pure, embodying the idea of the continuity of the soul, there being no real death in Spirit. Encouraging us to awake to the love and light within ourselves, he admonished us not to judge: 'Who will throw the first stone?' Amazingly, it is this religion that has most come to represent impossible rules of behavior creating guilt, shame, and separation. It is Christianity that teaches a child he is evil and his body sinful. It is this religion of 'love' that requires us to perform acts of redemption in order to earn God's love and attain salvation. And, to top it off, that salvation is unattainable through ourselves. We have to gain it through the church, the priest, or the Pope who is God's representative on earth.

Is there anyone who is not a representative of God on earth? Think about that! Think about what that kind of teaching has created in the psyche's of impressionable young children.

I knew a crusty Irish Catholic Priest who told me, 'If the Catholic Church has a child until six years old, it will be for life.' He knew the politics of control and was not popular in the church for that reason.

Recently, I saw a TV interview with a Catholic Archbishop commenting on the Pope's visit to the U.S. He talked about how moved he was to see God there in the Pope's presence. I felt rage rise up in me. 'Is God not in me and in every person watching this show?' Such a blanket denial of each of us! Most frighteningly, we have grown so used to this kind of belief, we do not even think twice about it. We suffer from the numbness of degradation.

Because we are so filled with beliefs of our unworthiness, when a great leader or teacher comes along, we think of them as separate or special, even if they are teaching oneness. We enjoy making heroes of people and then following them, in some hope of gaining their favor, and indirectly, God's favor. I am not saying we cannot acknowledge a teacher's wisdom and learn from them, but because of our great hunger for spiritual connection, we make these people our 'gods,' and we become lesser beings by definition.

I have met many wonderful people associated with different religions. I have worked with nuns who have a purity of heart, priests who really care about people, and ministers and rabbis who are committed to serving God. The path to enlightenment can come in many different ways and I truly acknowledge this. It can even happen in the church! Mother Teresa has been one of my teachers in her profound commitment to living unconditional love.

But the Divine Self is always here. It is not anywhere else, and not outside ourselves, as is usually taught in churches. No one person has more of the Self than anyone else, and we do not have to do anything to get it. **We are it.** We just have to see it and realize the truth of our own being. It is so easy and so natural.

So, what has happened? Why have the teachings of the greatest spiritual leaders on this planet become so distorted? Why have the revelations of love, forgiveness, oneness, and connectedness been so butchered? Why has so much death and misery followed the enlightenment of our greatest masters? That is a heavy question, and one I have been pondering for many years as a student of spirituality and human nature.

What I have concluded, is twofold; we suffer from ignorance

and emotional pain. Because we have had so little understanding of our emotional bodies, we have been overrun with our needs. Feeling powerless in our lives, we have tried to gain power in whatever way we could, most often at the expense of others. Feeling superior to others and telling ourselves we alone held the truth made us feel special and good about ourselves. We could justify brutal treatment of other groups by saying to ourselves, 'They deserve it; they are inferior to me: subhuman, not worthy of living.' Perceptually, we saw people different from ourselves as a threat. Biology is also involved here. In primitive tribes, a person who acted differently could endanger the survival of the group. So some of the fear around people having different beliefs is in our genetic make-up.

However, the desire for power is the big one. Power is what has motivated us human beings to control other human beings. It has allowed us to close our hearts and do unspeakables to one another. During the Crusades, it was considered a noble virtue to 'kill the heathens.' Telling on your neighbors and friends during the Inquisition was encouraged. In Ireland today it is patriotic for Catholics to kill Protestants, or vice versa.

Such madness, it takes one's breath away! All in the name of the church.

Still today church leaders try to control our personal lives and presume to tell us what is right and wrong: how to dress, who to associate with, what sexual practices to use, what sexual gender is the right one; who is going to hell and who to heaven. There is a basic psychological principle operating here. If we have denied our own freedom, then we do not want anyone else to be free either.

Control of others is a heady business. It can be very intoxicating, very addictive. It fills us with a rush of energy that is stimulating and exciting. We have the opportunity to experience a sense of importance that we do not normally feel in other areas of our lives. Having many people look up to us for direction and answers can assuage our insecurities and fill a void deep inside us, even if only temporarily. For awhile we can pretend that we are in charge, infallible, and indestructible. Ironically, we **are** all these things; we do not have to do anything to get them. They sit in our very own hearts.

Allowing other people to control us has come from ignorance. Not understanding the truth of our own emotional nature — that happiness is our innate state of being — we have believed contrary things told us by others. We thought they knew more about our truth than ourselves, about what we needed to be happy and fulfilled: we deferred to our parents, teachers, priests and politicians.

In order to acknowledge ourselves now, we are going to have to realize we have been fed some serious untruths. This realization will not be easy for us since it necessitates turning our current reality upside down. It can call into question other beliefs about ourselves and realities we have accepted as true, creating a ripple effect in our lives. But what can emerge on the other side is our unshakable belief in ourselves, and awareness of the power and love inside. This shaking up can be a wondrous awakening to inner freedom, our true power.

Taking a few steps back to view the bigger picture, we can see what has really been going on for the past several thousand years in relation to religion. Nobody is bad, although bad things have been done. We have been playing out a major planetary drama that is teaching us about who we are. I have observed that one of the major ways the divine intelligence teaches us is to show us what does not work. That seems to be the case here:  What happens when we give away our power to know our own truth? What happens when we give others the authority to dictate our daily lives? What happens when we are faced with guilty accusations about our worth and value? Where does it take us?

Only down. As we raise ourselves off the floor, we are ready to re-claim Self. No one knows what we need, or how to live our lives but ourselves. Others can only help us to the extent they point the way back to our own hearts. It is only here, in the silence of our own happiness, that truth lives. The charade is over. We are ready to be free. We already are...

# Sexuality: The Silent Hum of the Universe

'though modest and small,
a blossom has all the qualities
of an explosion'
— *Colette*

Orgasm is how we get here, and orgasm is how we leave here. That fast electrical frequency is the closest we humans come to experiencing God. Because of that, it has been a main focus of control and domination by leaders who did not want the average person to have such direct access to their own divinity.

It is also why so much fuss has been made over sexuality. In our longing to return home, to experience the frequency of the Divine Self, we have run after sexuality. We have abused it, and made it an object of bargaining. Women have used sexuality to gain freedom, to feel powerful, to ensure security and love. Men have viewed women as objects to be bargained for and possessed.

All of us have known that somehow the frequency of orgasm is magical, mysterious. We are transcended into realms of pleasure, vibrancy, and wholeness that we rarely touch in our daily lives. Sexuality can nourish us on the deepest levels of our being. It also allows for physical closeness and intimacy which helps to dispel our existential loneliness as a species.

Religions and cultures have known the power of sexuality and have manipulated it to serve their own purposes. In ancient times, virgins were sacrificed to appease the gods. Even today in some African tribes, a young girl's clitoris is cut off at puberty minimizing her pleasure from intercourse and ensuring her total availability to satisfy her future husband's needs. She will be his property. In the Christian tradition, not only is sexuality carefully structured — only in marriage, only in a certain way — control has gone even deeper to regulating the body itself. The church has judged the body and its desires to be 'of the devil,' or 'sins of the flesh.' It has succeeded in creating guilt of a magnitude unimaginable. Who of us feels totally comfortable with masturbation or intercourse? And what about all the variations? If we do feel at ease with our own sexuality, it is usually only after much therapeutic work on ourselves.

The women's movement has been a great help in encouraging all of us to re-claim our sexuality and pleasure in our physical bodies, to learn to love and care for our bodies as the miracles of life they are.

The body is the expression of the divine in physical form. If we deny the body, then we deny the expression of our soul's purpose. We are here in a body, nowhere else. This is it; we are it. We are the incredible experiment called human. Let us live it, love it, and re-claim our birthright of ecstasy.

When we stand in the divine flow, we experience a current that is electrical, light, and orgasmic. When we deepen into this current, we feel bliss and peace. A deep pleasure permeates our body. It is sexual. We are sexual. The sexual frequency is the current of life. It vibrates the color in every flower; it is the bird's song. It moves the breeze. It is the same vibrancy radiating from children that makes us want to caress them. Touching a plant is sexual, as is viewing a sunset. To deny our sexuality is to deny life itself.

# Meditation, etc.

———————————— ∞ ————————————

Meditation is really just a way to still the mind. It is simple, direct and easily accessible. It costs nothing and requires no special equipment. There are meditation techniques and styles to fit everyone. Every religious tradition has meditation practices of some kind, call it prayer or just being silent.

Sometimes mantras are used: words said over and over in a repetitive manner. Its goal is to give the mind something to focus on — occupy itself — while the deeper Self is revealed. Some feel that mantras hold special energy that help a person align with the divine frequency. Saying one's mantra over and over allows consciousness to expand.

Focusing on a particular image is another popular meditative technique. For centuries people have focused on Jesus, the Virgin Mother, Buddha, and other saints embodying the energies of love, compassion, and peace. Truly it is all very scientific. The mind has such great power: whatever it focuses its attention on becomes real for that person. Ancients knew the techniques, they just had different explanations for the reasons. It is all the same: finding ways to quiet the mind so the inner radiance can be felt.

The problem with some of these tools is that they have become institutionalized, rigid, and lifeless. We are made to feel guilty if we do not practice them regularly. They have turned into goals in and of themselves: saying confession, going to church twice a week, eating certain foods, mastering yogic techniques, and abstinence from sex, alcohol, music, and dance. Even in less traditional New Age circles, meditation and diet often turn into 'shoulds.' I have observed that many of these practices started out with an understanding of truth but lost their original intent as the years went by. Or, they became distorted by their leaders for the purpose of control.

A few years ago in Paris, I went to High Mass at the Notre Dame Cathedral one Sunday morning. It was incredibly beautiful. I was caught up in the spectacle of priests in flowing white robes and decorative red hats, the choir of young male voices echoing through this magnificent structure and the sense of reverence in the people present. I am not a Catholic, but I could easily relate to the sentiments of love and charity expressed by the Archbishop as he spoke of the upcoming Christmas season.

When people approached the altar to take the wafer and drink the wine for communion, I got it! I understood what the church is doing with that ritual. By taking in symbolically, (also energetically), the body and blood of Christ, this activity allows the body to align with the frequencies that Christ represents; love, light, joy, and compassion. Apparently some persons in the very beginning of this religion, understood the laws of energy.

I realized that many of the Church's rituals are designed to open the body and calm the mind through repetitious prayer, incense, and music. Sadly, I also saw where the Church has strayed from its original teachings. It has focused on the death of Jesus and his suffering, rather than his true message of love and compassion. My eyes scanned this towering Cathedral, showing macabre paintings of Christ's death. The message conveyed: 'he died for our sins and we should feel guilty.' And we do... The practice of confession is also based on truth. If we can talk about our feelings and know we are forgiven, we can feel better psychologically. Problematically, it is the church itself that has taught us to feel guilty in the first place! Then, it puts itself in the position of 'forgiving' us. It's a pretty good game.

Some church practices include passionate singing and 'speaking in tongues.' These activities can produce an altered state, where the mind lets go. At that time, deeper wisdom and understanding can come forth, even healing. 'Let go and let God' is not an empty proverb. Just the idea of kneeling before an altar can produce a humbling, a sense of awe at the magnificence of the divine. It can create a moment, an instant, where we let go, and know we are much more.

I have heard many people say that nature is their church. There, they can commune with the inner silence that permeates the trees, water, sky, and animals. They can feel the pulsation that is ever present. It calms and rejuvenates them.

Peace can be found in many places for different people. For some, it is on the golf course or the tennis court, perhaps fishing on a river. It can be felt by looking out a window, or staring into a fire. Peace can be found in the middle of a huge city street if the attention is on the inner silence.

I am suggesting that there is a way to experience peace and happiness with or without an activity or ritual. Since we do not really need to 'do' anything, any activity or practice we are drawn to can be useful if done with the awareness that it is a tool and not a substitute for the real thing. Its purpose is to point the way back to ourselves, where ultimately everything resides.

An example of the limitations of ritualized meditation is the Hindu story of an elephant and its owner walking through the marketplace. Because it is the nature of the elephant to swing its unoccupied trunk back and forth, the owner gives the trunk a stick to keep it from doing damage as they walk through the marketplace together. When they reach the edge of town, the owner retrieves the stick and the trunk begins to swing again. The teaching: techniques used to quiet the mind, such as mantras, concentration, songs, etc. have a limited function. They work for awhile but then the mind kicks in again when the practice is over. Their efficacy is limited. It's better to see 'who is aware' when the mind is busy and when it is still, and put the attention there. That requires no effort, no technique, rather a shift in focus.

## BREAKING OLD HABITS

Sometimes change is a practical matter of breaking old habits and requires very practical solutions. Along with doing the necessary work in understanding and clearing our emotional bodies, we may also need help in finding new ways to respond to life. Often, the destructive patterns continue because new behavior has not yet been learned to replace the old. It's almost mechanical, as if we need to learn new styles of thinking. It seems we are stuck in a rut of reaction and response.

There are many beneficial systems that can help a person in de-programming and learning new behaviors, Alcoholics Anonymous being perhaps the best known. There are numerous programs which offer structures for changing behavior and teaching practical skills along the way. Repeating affirmations is also helpful in refocusing the mind. In my experience, it usually takes forty days to change a behavior.

I find both kinds of work to be necessary; doing the underlying energetic clearing and learning new ways to think, feel and act.

Whatever works.

# The Arts

---∞---

A few years ago, while contemplating a dive into and surrender to my great passion painting, the awareness came to me that the next wave of transformation on the planet would come through the arts: poetry, literature, painting, sculpture, music, dance and drama. These expressions increase our vibrations on the inner levels bypassing the mind, which is slower to change. Because our species is speeding up, we now need more holistic, comprehensive ways to reach all levels of our being.

## POETRY

### Poetry

And it was at that age ... Poetry arrived
in search of me. I don't know, I don't know where
it came from, from winter or a river.
I don't know how or when,
no, they were not voices, they were not
words, nor silence,
but from a street I was summoned,
from the branches of night,
abruptly from the others,
among violent fires
or returning alone,
there I was without a face
and it touched me.

I did not know what to say, my mouth
had no way
with names,
my eyes were blind,
and something started in my soul,
fever or forgotten wings,
and I made my own way,
deciphering
that fire,
and I wrote the first faint line,
faint, without substance, pure
nonsense,
pure wisdom
of someone who knows nothing,
and suddenly I saw
the heavens
unfastened
and open,
planets,
palpitating plantations,
shadow perforated,
riddled
with arrows, fire and flowers,
the winding night, the universe.

And I, infinitesimal being,
drunk with the great starry
void,
Likeness, image of
mystery,
felt myself a pure part
of the abyss,
I wheeled with the stars,
my heart broke loose on the wind.
                — *Pablo Neruda*, Love, Ten Poems by Pablo Neruda[7]

Poetry is the media for madness and ecstasy. It goes into the vast open spaces of our consensus reality and brings back an altered awareness through its word-play. Poetry is one of the best ways to have an experience of other realities as you feel your consciousness lift, move, expand and open. Meaning cannot be grasped with the linear part of our minds: we have to engage our intuitive side that just 'feels' the nuances of meaning.

### Into Sun Again

The walls were stone, and cold
Yet held for me a mute attraction
Cut, as they were, by hand
And fitted without crevice,
Hard, clean, separate,
Wanting nothing but light.

Fearful
I groped without balance
Finally floating free
To find what I so long
Had searched for.

Darkness is not altogether ugly
Nor sight a perfect gift I guess
And I forget
How it was I came
From that black abyss
Into sun again.

— *Sandra Smith-Etigson*

Sri Aurbindo, an Eastern mystic, was deeply involved in observing and describing the evolution of the species which he could see on a cellular level in his meditations. After writing many philosophical books, he concluded that poetry was the best way to give the reader the actual experience of these new realities and shifts of awareness.

A light not born of the sun or moon or fire,
A light that dwelt within and saw within
Shedding an intimate visibility...

A million lotuses swaying on one stem,
World after coloured and ecstatic world
Climbs towards some far unseen epiphany.

To Sri Aurobindo, the word 'kavi' had a double meaning of 'seer of the Truth' and 'poet.' One was a poet because one was a seer.

The planes of consciousness are characterized not only by different intensities of luminous vibrations, but by different sound vibrations or rhythms one can hear when one has that 'ear of ear' the Veda mentions... The higher one rises, the more harmonious, unified and streamlined, the vibrations become, like certain great notes of Beethoven's string quartets, which seem to draw us upwards, breathlessly, to dazzling heights of pure light... The very frequency of vibration turns the rainbow of colors to pure white, to such a high pitch that it seems motionless, as if caught in eternity...

...There is a higher magic which also derives from handling vibrations, on higher planes of consciousness. This is poetry, music... In this case the sound holds in itself the power of experience and realization — it is a sound that makes one see.

Similarly, poetry and music, which are but an unconscious process of handling those secret vibrations, can be a powerful means of opening up the consciousness... True poetry is action, it opens up

little inlets in the consciousness, through which the
Real can enter.                                 — *Satprem*
    Sri Aurobindo or The Adventure of Consciousness[8]

## MUSIC

One afternoon, I had the great privilege of listening to classical
music with a friend of mine who is a talented orchestra conductor.
The music moved me to tears as I felt a great opening in my heart.
Somewhat apologetic, I looked over at this man, certain that he was
deep into intellectual examination of the music. He, too, had tears in his
eyes. When I told him that I always felt music in my body as vibration, he
gently assured me, 'That's how music is meant to be experienced.'

From W.A. Mathieu's book, *The Musical Life*[9]

When you listen to music, it goes where no
one else goes but you. It reverberates in a chamber so
secret that even you can't go there without giving yourself special permission.

...Listening to music is like a wedding ceremony where
everyone gets married to everyone else. Every mem-
ber of the party has the same desire: to turn into music, to live as the entwined vibrations coursing the
space in this split second. When the ceremony is at its
peak and the magic has broken loose, every beat in
every bar says: this is who we **are**, this, **this**, is who we
are, on and on, in every stroke.

And on opera,

Operatic drama, extravagant as it often is, neverthe-
less lives tenaciously from generation to generation,
and appears in culture after culture. We love to see

ourselves proscenium-boxed and choreographed-
sculpted as singing gods, hurling forth our deepest secret in magnificent arias, while the assembled bands
and choruses approve, condemn, and egg us on. What
if you opened your eyes only to discover that you and
your friends were on stage in an opera, midscene?
There are no special costumes or sets. The scenery is
what you see now, the costumes what you are wearing now. There is no score: the music consists of the
sounds you are hearing now.

Well said...

## DANCE
Folklore tells of a French king who instructed his minister to come
up with a dance that would remind him of angels. The ballet was born.
I first went to a ballet at the age of ten and was totally enchanted.
I could feel something lifting and moving those flowing bodies, effortlessly, gracefully. The costumes, sets and music all felt light, joyful, supernatural. I fell in love. I realize now, I was tuning into the
energy of angels, or perhaps remembering the innate lightness of my
own being.
To me, dance demonstrates the unlimited resources of our physical expression, showing what's possible for us. We can soar, leap, fly,
spin, stretch — separately and together in simultaneous rapture.

## ART
Where to begin? Painting is the heart of my being, the place I go
for absolute joy, where I revel in the life force coming through me as
it continually expresses and creates new forms. I see the act of painting as standing in the direct current of the divine being, at one with
the cosmic act of creation. Pure delight.
Artistic expression has been many things for many people. That
is the beauty of art. It is so personal and universal at the same time,

one's unique expression.

Famous painters have spoken with reverence about their creative process. Picasso would 'take off my ego, along with my shoes' when entering his studio, where 'something else' took over. And we see the results. We recognize in great art its vital themes and energies that stay alive from generation to generation. There's a familiar resonance about these masterpieces beyond the skill and mastery of the artist. Although great craftsmen come and go, it is the essence or quality of the energy that seems to guarantee immortality. It has to have that special something that speaks to our hearts.

Hildegard, a Benedictine nun who was a 12th century Christian mystic and physician, felt that an important aspect of healing was the use of art, believing it is the artist's special role to be the awakener of the people. Carl Jung was fascinated with art and the creative process, claiming that artists were the closest people to God. Quite a statement! Yet, I find it to be true in my life. When I'm in my studio, I enter the timeless present where all problems drop away. I need only to stay in that flow and I am guided and inspired: painting — pure ecstasy.

Anyone can paint, or do some form of artistic expression. When I first began painting 20 years ago, I was blessed with a very unique teacher who taught one day a week at the Officers Club at Wright-Patterson Air Force Base in Dayton, Ohio. She was a local college professor and her goal was to introduce us to all media of artistic expression: oil and acrylic painting, which included realism; hard-edge and abstract expressionism; collage; sculpture; and nude figure drawing. Figure drawing was quite controversial in Middle America in those days. I remember her bringing a bottle of wine to class one day to 'loosen us up.' I painted a purple nude that day...

In fact, as an art teacher, she found the hardest things for her students was their need to 'do it right,' or draw inside the lines. She was constantly encouraging us to play and have fun. She believed there was a genius in each one of us, that we just needed to find the right vehicle for that artistic expression. What a great gift her teaching gave us.

I did indeed find my niche — a love of color and a fluidity with different dimensions; I also found a freedom of expression that surprised and delighted me. I have come to see painting as another level of my healing work. The greatest compliment I can receive is when people say my paintings carry joy and make them feel good.

In France a few years ago, I had great fun painting the beautiful countryside, absolutely inspired by the tradition of the French Impressionists. One might say I was in 'hog heaven.'

A friend of mine, a gentle woman of German birth, came to visit me one day while I was painting. She was very silent as I threw paint on the canvas in great abandon while Jazz music bounced from the radio. Later, eyes wide she said to me, 'I didn't know you could just paint whatever you want. I thought there were rules...'

No rules. We just need to play. Children know this. Such fun to express ourselves.

And so healing.

## THEATRE ARTS

Movies, television, novels and plays are where it's all happening. Our lives are continually being shaped by the extravaganza of stories, entertainment, fashion, personalities and lifestyles. It is a most profound influence in our lives, whether or not we like it, and that influence is on a global scale.

If we pay close attention to the underlying currents, we can pick up themes and energies being expressed and explored on a cellular level. We are using these media for shifting consciousness. Along with playing out our primal impulses of sex and violence, we are seeing movies and TV programs that remind us to love ourselves and each other. When I heard that *Forrest Gump* had won the Academy Award for best picture one year, I said to myself, 'with all the violence and alienation in society, people are wanting to feel the simple beauty and power of love.'

For the first time in this planet's history, we are globally joined by communication satellites; we can send and receive information at the same time. We're coming closer to simultaneous communication, the metaphor of our collective unconscious.

What power this affords us to expand our consciousness! The movie producer Stephen Spielberg opened the hearts and minds of audiences in his movie *E.T.* allowing us a view of aliens as being like us on the inner levels, having the same concerns for 'home.' Gene Roddenberry evoked the heroic possibilities of humankind, combining technology with inner wisdom in his ground breaking TV series *Star Trek.* In the most violent movies, one may gain insight into the pain or madness that precipitated these acts. I am even optimistic about horror movies. I feel we are looking at our species' dark/shadow side so it can be healed.

Ultimately, the power of the theatre arts is its capacity to entertain. We don't want to be lectured or told what to do; we want to be entertained. Through that process, inner change can come of its own accord, naturally. This is its greatest power.

Shakespeare knew it...

## LITERATURE

In childhood reading novels saved my life. Through the magic of the written word and my imagination, I was able to reach out to a wider world than was around me. I was able to know about relationships and families that were happy and loving, about distant places, time periods and cultures. I learned to dream, exploring the possibilities of character, costume and drama — all in the intimacy of my own bedroom. A romantic novel is a delightful escape.

To this day, novels are 'delicious' to me. They offer a way to move, to learn and have the privilege of seeing into other hearts and minds. I don't feel so alone in the cosmos knowing other people are having experiences comparable to mine. A good mystery or science fiction story allows me to enter the fascinating workings of the human mind and to enlarge my experience in this great adventure of life.

Literature opens the windows to inner and outer worlds. It's almost as good as past-life sessions!

# The Infinite: Do We Dare?

Going within involves touching the formless, the eternal silent presence from which everything emerges and to which everything returns. Realizing this impartial yet deeply personal presence, we gain access to unimaginable power and love. This is all available ... now... with no effort.

It seems so preposterous, so unbelievable to us! 'How can one know and trust the unseen?' the mind asks. In truth, experiences of a deeper reality are beyond the accustomed paths of our minds. They do not fit our learned paradigm that external is the only reality. It seems obvious to the physical senses that we are alone in separate bodies, so how can anything invisible or transcendent really be true? Our belief in separation underlies these issues.

Scientists have helped us realize that, while we have separate physical bodies, the substance of these bodies is pure light/energy, all of the same essence. We are different branches of the same tree, made of the same material. But in order to really know this inside, to make it real for us, a perceptual shift has to be made. If we look with our inner vision, we can see the light, radiant vibration in people around us. We can feel/sense/know these different energy currents as expressed in nature and all of life. We can re-train our minds to look past and under the visible world to the underlying truth. To really live our lives from this place, these knowings, involves taking a leap, a deepening of trust in something supported by neither our larger culture nor our individual programming.

God. The Divine. What is it? Why anything? The mind asks these questions over and over. It wants to understand. But the divine force cannot be known through the mind. The answers come from having direct experience of it: in the surrender.

When surrender happens it is so different, so strange. It is as if the contents of life's events no longer matter. One is in a state of being, a clear, intense, rich vibration that is a 'click in consciousness.' It is only found in the present moment: the silence that holds peace, bliss, excitement. It feels completely unlike ordinary life. Clicking into the divine stream can seem so difficult and yet be so easy, can feel so strange and yet so familiar. Can this be it? Is there anywhere else to go? One wonders, do other people know this? Can they feel it? Do they care?

We move up against confrontation with 'God' and then we back away. It is vast ... so awesome. It is easier to distract ourselves with TV, mental obsessions, relationships and activities, for we know we will change profoundly if we open to this power. One day, however, we come to a point in our lives where connection to Source is all that matters and our focus turns to direct experience of that underlying compassionate presence that is always with us. We only desire direct experience of our deepest Self. We wish to be whole again.

Wholeness is what we have searched for in love relationships and what has ultimately remained unfulfilled. It is that great love totally filling the heart, the direct experience of everlasting purpose, the intelligent undercurrent of life — with every moment, every word. It is conscious, alive awareness. We want to know this, not just occasionally as a meditative practice, but to be immersed in that loving presence every second.

# Love

*"The power of a true heart is immense."*
— Sri Nisargadatta Maharaj

Pure, sweet unconditional love. We have yearned to feel and know this love all our lives. As children, we desperately searched the faces of our parents and those around us, looking, for approval. More to the point, we were looking for the way it made us feel: happy, warm, nourished and complete. Love brings total well-being, a joy that begins in our hearts and spreads through our bodies.

As children, most of us did not know this feeling very often. Our parents were unhappy and frustrated with themselves and each other. Even as embryos, we picked up our parents' emotional pain. By coming into life during and after World War II, the Korean or Vietnam War we took on major imprints of battle and fear that were in the planet's auric field. Whenever fear predominates, love is pushed aside.

Looking back on our lives, we can acknowledge that the desire for unconditional love has been a driving force in our lives, albeit, not always a conscious one. As we come to the realization that this love feeling is not something **to get**, but something **to be**, we can open to the love inside that has been waiting for us. We just have to 'tune the dial' to where this feeling/knowing lives. Some call it another dimension or frequency; some call it God.

I have come to see the process as **remembering**: remembering who we really are, what sits inside us as the underlying substance of all things. Remembering what has always been there, what has never left. It is the vibration in our hearts that brings tears of joy, the ecstatic radiance of pure bliss. So deep, it is the background music of life. We only have to tune into it to be enveloped. And the acceptance! It is truly beyond our comprehension that we could be loved so totally and completely. Love. Every moment. If we could only have known.

We can feel love welling up inside us throughout the day. We can also call it in purposefully or simply stop to feel it. The feeling can be so tender, rich and full.  Complete. Best of all, we do not have to earn it. It sits inside our hearts huge like a shining sun. The love feeling can be continuous as we re-identify ourselves as this love. We have always known this love was possible. We never dreamed that **we** were it, and that it could be so easy...

What a joke!

If we are determined, it is possible to stay in this state. The loving presence within wants to merge and be alive in our lives as the only reality. As we abide in the heart, a love pours forth that begins to melt barriers with people. Manipulation and fear drop away in clumps. There is nothing to get, and nothing to lose. It was never outside us: always inside waiting to be re-kindled, awakened, remembered...

# Awareness

There is a place where all techniques fall away. Pure awareness. Simple awareness. Radiant awareness.

When we have grown tired of our stories and dramas — removed some of the charge and interest in them — we are ready for something else: ready to just be. Then, we become conscious of a silent awareness behind and beneath everything; every thought, movement, event, person, place. We turn our attention to this and abide there. It is the eternal silence, emptiness; the beingness that is aware of the observer and the observed.

When we sink into this, there comes a vibrant glow, peace, joy. We are in direct contact with the substance of the universe. There is nothing to strive for or attain. In this place, nothing needs to be denied. It is what is aware of all our experiences and what creates us moment by moment: the wise silence that sits behind our thoughts. The eternal permanence that never dies, that has temporarily taken form as us.

We touch a current of energy, loving beyond our comprehension. Ecstasy is its essential nature, a burning radiance containing the power of All That Is. It is we. We are it. We have never been separate; we have just focused on other things.

In this realization, life is lived in the present moment with harmony, wisdom, and love. Our repetitive thoughts fade away as we withdraw interest. Our ego/emotional body now becomes fascinated with something else; exploring this magnificent presence, stillness. Merging with divine radiance is much more delicious than anything ego has known before.

Life is rich; every moment is sacred, precious. Every person and event is created by this vast awareness, this magnificent silence. Fear is gone. What is to fear when one is aligned with the permanent reality? Since there can be no death, the pain of separation dissolves along with the loneliness. We are merged forever in the divine awareness that is the mystery of the universe. It is glorious beyond belief! One understands what the saints and mystics have been saying for centuries.

To know the divine directly, just ask the question, 'Who am I?' Then ask, who is aware of that question? What is the silence before and after that question, or in between our thoughts? Now begins a whole new exploration based on 'being,' deepening into awareness of Self. Every moment.

## 'I AM THAT'

The mystics tell us we are not our bodies, we are not our emotions and we are not our thoughts. The true essence of us includes all of that but lies beyond that. Enlightenment comes when we can live in the silence beyond, in pure awareness.

We don't have to leave life in order to do this. We can still enjoy the body, emotions, thinking — our dramas — but in a way that is playful. Consciousness has taken on these human forms to have an experience, and we are not here to deny that experience; rather to see what is truly real and permanent. As we deepen into the silence surrounding and infusing every moment, we come to a peaceful space beyond understanding, a richness and fullness that contains everything we have always wanted. It is what we have traditionally called God, but far beyond our human concepts.

The Indian Saint Ramana Maharshi became enlightened at the age of 17. He experienced a sudden fear of death so he laid down on the floor of his bedroom and said to himself, 'OK let's see what it would be like to go beyond the body senses, the thinking mind and the emotions. Is there anything there?' And he found the stillness, the pure spaciousness and incredible ecstatic love which lives there eternally. He then left his home and devoted his life to deepening into 'that' and sharing it with the world.

We don't have to go anyplace or do anything in order to experience Self. It is here now. It is what is aware of this page, processing these thoughts. Always, eternally aware.

In life, enlightenment brings a sense of peace and serenity to whatever we are doing, a spontaneous knowing that doesn't have to be planned. There is ease, a lack of worry as we trust the inner wisdom and intelligence to be there. Even when we react to life out of our emotional patterns, the focus is on 'who is aware' of our reactions. Who is always there, whether we are happy or sad? From where did the thought arise? Attention is removed from the thoughts and behaviors themselves and focused deeper. 'Who is aware of this?' Then life can be lived as it is lived. No need to hide or withdraw. Simply being one with the awareness; we are finally free.

# The Adventure

———————————————————⟨∞⟩———————————————————

So ... now what? — the mind asks. As we cross the threshold into identification with pure awareness, it is a whole new ball game, and we know it. That's one of the reasons we have been avoiding this inner silence. We know intuitively that once we enter this space, we are in new territory. We haven't been ready until now. What does it mean to 'be still and know God?' What is 'out there' or 'in here?' Who will we be? What will we find? What is this underlying intelligence that is eternal, never dies?

I think of my favorite TV program *Star Trek*, 'to boldly go where no one has gone before.' It is that time. We are on the threshold of something so new and exciting that we cannot grasp the scope, the possibilities that are awaiting this exploration of consciousness. It is the new frontier.

As we identify with the silent current of the Self, so many things drop away: fear, worry, and control are unnecessary. Something else benevolent and wise is guiding the show. Analyzing and figuring out become silly activities; just something to occupy the mind, but not a way to find truth. Ego and the separate self take their place as an interesting drama, but certainly not all there is. Our attention is now drawn to what arouses a deep-felt interest or passion in the heart, to what creates peace, joy, aliveness. We fall in love with **that**. We begin to want to spend time with our truest love, seeking intimacy as with our human lovers in the first stages of romantic love. We are fascinated, intrigued, awed; we can't get enough. Wonderfully, the

Divine Self can give us all that we have longed for in a lover — and so much more. And it never leaves us.

As we place our interest and attention on the inner silence, we become aware of its rhythms, vibrations, its tenderness and love. Every moment is full and complete. Knowings and understandings arise spontaneously. 'To know it is to be it' takes on profound meaning. And we are just dipping our toes into the ocean of awareness. What possibilities await us as we walk further into the water. What unimaginable adventures and experiences!

This is where we are now.

The true adventure begins.

Let the curtain rise...

# NOTES

1. From *Ageless Body, Timeless Mind* by Deepak Chopra, M.D. ©1993. Harmony Books, Crown Publisher, Inc. New York, N.Y.

2. From *Be As You Are, The Teachings of Sri Ramana Maharshi*, edited by David Godman, ©1992. Penguin Books USA, Inc., New York, N.Y.

3. From *I Am That* by Sri Nisargadatta Maharaj, ©1973. The Acorn Press, Durham, N.Y.

4. From *The Book of Runes* by Ralph H. Blum, ©1993. St. Martin's Press, New York, N.Y.

5. From *A Return To Love* by Marianne Williamson, ©1993. HarperCollins.

6. From *The Abundance Book* by John Randolph Price, ©1983,1996. Hay House, Inc., Carlsbad, CA. Used by permission.

7. From *Love, Ten Poems by Pablo Neruda*, ©1969. Miramax Books, Hyperion, New York, N.Y.

8. From *Sri Aurobindo, or The Adventure of Consciousness* by Satprem, ©1984. Institute for Evolutionary Research, New York, N.Y.

9. From *The Musical Life* by W.A. Mathieu, ©1994. Reprinted by arrangement with Shambhala Publications, Inc., 300 Massachusetts Avenue, Boston, MA 02115.

## THE NETWORK

Since 1994, Susan Harris has been training individuals through-out the world to be facilitators in Multi-Incarnational Therapy. These facilitators have formed a Network which is involved with referral, publishing a newsletter, exchanging information, ongoing training, and general support. They can be found in different cities in Canada, Europe, and the United States. Information may be obtained by contacting:

**The Network**
c/o Susan Harris
P.O. Box 9939
Santa Fe, New Mexico 87504-9939
Tel: 505.984.1274
Fax: 505.984.8410

Susan is currently available for talks and workshops and offers facilitator trainings twice a year. She can be reached at the above address.

ORDERING INFORMATION

# Theater of the Soul:
## *The Higher Self and Multi-Incarnational Exploration*

1 copy: $12.95 each
2-10 copies: $11.50 each
11 -20 copies: $10.25 each
20 + copies: $9.00 each

Please include $2.50 per book for shipping and handling.

Order direct from:
**Wind Horse Publications**
P.O. Box 9939
Santa Fe, NM 87504-9939

Tel: 505.984.1274
Fax: 505.984.8410